To our clients, who are always generous with their feedback, especially when we are wrong.

Contents

Introduction

History never repeats itself; but it often rhymes.

This simple fact explains why so many financial analysts, market strategists and portfolio managers like to study past economic cycles and market reactions before taking investment decisions. By studying financial and economic history, market participants are able to anchor beliefs on solid facts.

For over ten years now, a wide majority of market strategists and economists from respected investment banks (Morgan Stanley, Dresdner…), a large number of upscale financial publications (*The Economist, The Financial Times*…), highly respected consulting firms (*Lombard Street Research, Grant's Interest Rate Observer, Gloom Boom Doom*…) have drawn on historical parallels to warn us that the expansion of the past decade in US consumption was both unsustainable and likely to end in tears. Real estate all over the Christian civilised world was bound to collapse, along with global equity markets. The world would then enter into an 'ice age'. So far, despite the strength of the above thought process, and the numerous historical parallels, the dreaded meltdown has completely failed to materialise. So what is the next step?

When a thought process fails, i.e., when history fails to rhyme, money managers and analysts can typically respond in one of four ways:

1) Shut up and crawl under the carpet. This is usually an expensive proposition.

2) Pretend that the numbers are wrong and that, despite all the signs, they are right (i.e., enter into denial). This too, is an expensive proposition.

3) Hope that one is simply 'early' and that one's scenario is about to unfold. This can sometimes work, but more often than not, proves costly. Moreover, after ten years of predicting Armageddon, one's credibility tends to melt away.

4) Admit that one has been wrong, and try to find out where the mistakes lie. This is the most intellectually honest stance to take and the one that we wish to adopt in the following pages. After all, as Churchill once said, 'an economist needs to be able to forecast what is going to happen in a week, a month, and a year, and then be able to explain why it did not'.

The reason so many analysts drag their feet in admitting that history has failed to rhyme this time around is that it would lead one to the dreaded conclusion that 'things are different this time'. But why is this a dreaded conclusion? Because anyone who has spent ten minutes on a trading floor knows that saying 'things are different this time' is:

1) the easiest way to get laughed out of a room,

2) the most expensive words ever pronounced,

3) the surest way to lose any kind of credibility,

And yet, this is exactly what we aim to argue in the following pages.

Arguing that 'things are different this time', we freely admit that we might end up drawing the wrong conclusions, say silly things and establish relationships where there are none. We also realise that some of our more cynical clients (say those sitting in Boston or London), might read the coming chapters and conclude that we have really been drinking the Kool-Aid. These are the risks when one ventures into uncharted territory. We accept these risks gladly, for we are convinced that the first step to successful investing is an understanding of the current world.

Unfortunately, History is of little help to this understanding. We have to draw solely on logic, and the help of our friends and clients. With this in mind, we kindly ask that you contact us if you see a flaw in any of the arguments that we present. Again, this is a work in progress, the final aim of which is to help us understand the world we live in so that we can deploy our capital more efficiently.

Beyond logic, and our experiences, we have a third pillar to rely on: the great writings of living, and dead, economists. Throughout this book, we will lean heavily on the works of past intellectual giants, such as Modigliani, Fisher, Schumpeter, Bastiat and Ricardo. In that sense, we are like dwarves sitting on top of the heads of giants; thanks to them, we can see just a bit further.

One such intellectual giant is Alvin Toffler. In his books, Alvin Toffler describes three types of societies, based on the concept of 'waves' – where each wave pushes the older societies and cultures aside. The 'First Wave' was the society that followed the agrarian revolution and replaced the first hunter-gatherer cultures. The 'Second Wave' was based on industrial mass production, mass distribution, mass consumption, mass education, mass media, mass recreation, mass entertainment, and weapons of mass destruction. The 'Third Wave' is the post-industrial society. In this post-industrial society, there is a lot of diversity in lifestyles ('subcults'). Adhocracies (fluid organisations like GaveKal) adapt quickly to changes. Information can substitute most of the material resources and becomes the main material for workers (cognitarians instead of proletarians), who are loosely affiliated. Mass customisation offers the possibility of cheap, personalised production catering to small niches. The gap between producer and consumer is bridged by technology. 'Prosumers' can fill their own needs…

To the reader today, all the above seems pretty evident. But what is quite impressive is that Toffler wrote *Future Shock* in 1970 and *The Third Wave* in 1980. What is depressing, however, is that the dismal science has yet to adjust to the world of the Third Wave. Indeed, wherever you care to look, economists are talking about industrial production numbers, inventory levels, trade balances ... When all these measures, for Third Wave economies, are increasingly becoming irrelevant.

In a sense, economists today are the mirror image of the very first economists: the physiocrats. Back in the late XVIIIth century, the physiocrats (Quesnay, Dupont de Nemours ...) explained how value-added could only come from agriculture (you planted a seed, and got a plant). They were 'first-wave' economists, completely blind to the entire economic re-organisation of the industrial revolution taking off in front of their eyes. They could easily see that agriculture created value, but could not see that the value created by industry would dwarf that of agriculture.

Today, as the physiocrats before them, too many market participants are stuck in previous-wave thinking mode and miss the current social and economic revolution. As Toffler predicted, successful companies no longer operate on the business models used a generation ago. Relationships between countries have evolved. Social structures are transforming themselves at a rapid pace.

In short, the world has changed. So shouldn't our way of analysing it evolve as well? Why should we shy away from exclaiming that 'things are different this time'? In the following pages, we aim to look at what we believe are the important differences. And what they mean for our political organisations and the financial markets.

We are entering into a Brave New World.

A new business model – the platform company

We were stunned. Entering onto the trading floor of the treasury department of one of our industrial clients, we felt that we could have been on the floor of any large investment bank. On our left were guys in the midst of complicated financial arbitrage operations. Straight ahead, the fixed-income team seemed busy deciphering the latest Greenspanisms. On our right, we were greeted with open arms and asked: 'so, what do you guys see in store for the future'.

A truthful answer would have been, 'you tell us – you guys are making it!' Unfortunately, that's probably not the answer for which our client paid us generously. So instead, we went through our Investment Strategy Chart Book, discussing what the Fed might do next, the potential for structural reforms from European governments, what was happening in China, etc.

But our heart was not in it. As we spoke, the future was being shaped by our client and the new breed of company he had created. And all the talk about monetary policy, fiscal discipline and the like was just that: talk. In the great scheme of things, the governments were becoming bit players in the revolution at hand. Companies were evolving. Business processes were being turned upside down. The workplace was changing. And all this would have a much greater long-term impact on the way financial markets, and politics, function than any of Mr Greenspan's declarations ever could.

Rewinding for a minute, it might be useful to review what companies have historically done. Up until recently, a typical company did the following: it designed a product, manufactured the product, and then sold the product. Take Ford for example. Ford designs an Expedition SUV. Ford manufactures the truck at a plant in Detroit. Ford then sends the truck on to a Ford dealership somewhere in the US to be sold.

This vertical design/produce/sell business model has been the model de rigueur for the past 50 years. Really successful companies followed this model at home, then abroad (i.e., Toyota). Companies became multinationals. Each multinational started as a purely domestic company, and eventually started to produce everywhere to sell wherever they were producing.

This was yesterday's business model.

The new business model is to produce nowhere, but sell everywhere. In recent years, we have witnessed the birth of a new breed of company that we shall call the 'platform company'. Platform companies know where the clients are and what they want and where the producers are. Platform companies then simply organise the ordering by the clients and the delivery by the producers (and the placing of their logo on the product just before delivery).

Platform companies keep the high added-value parts of research, development, treasury and marketing in-house, and farm out all the rest to external producers. Typical examples include Dell, Wal-Mart, IKEA, Hennes & Mauritz, Li & Fung and many others.

Indeed, an increasing number of Western companies are looking at their business models and saying: 'out of the three things I do – designing, producing and selling – producing is a mug's game. Producing ties up a lot of capital. It is often labour-intensive. It forces one to keep expensive inventories. It is highly volatile. And I do not get rewarded for it in the market place (manufacturing businesses typically trade at discounts to non-manufacturing businesses in the stock market, mostly because they are more volatile and offer lower returns on invested capital). I would be better off leaving the producing to some other mug, and focus on the non-cyclical, high value-added part of my business, namely designing and selling.'

An increasing number of companies have taken a look at their operations and have decided that the way to succeed is to operate on much leaner balance sheets. Take hotel companies as an example. Apart from Accor of France, most hotel companies around the world (Hilton, Marriott, etc.) have, or are trying, to shed assets. Instead of owning hotels, they simply manage them.

In micro-economic terms, this 'light balance sheet' model makes plenty of sense. It allows companies to act swiftly if/when a decision has been wrong. It is like travelling with a small backpack instead of travelling with a suite of trunks. One can change itinerary rapidly and avoid losses. When executed properly, the platform company business model makes for very high, and stable, returns on invested capital.

This new business model also has important economic, political, social and financial implications. But before we get to them, let us review the pillars on which the new platform company model rests; and whether these pillars are stable or not.

Is the 'platform company business model' here to stay?

The 'platform company business model' rests on four important pillars:

- *Free trade* (free trade allows platform companies to produce goods wherever production is attractively priced)

- *Technological progress*, especially in communications (technology allows platform companies to manage a creative process where design, production and sales are no longer centralised)

- *Recurrent overcapacity in most industries* (overcapacities allow platform companies to never run out of goods to sell)

- *Ability to move goods around without difficulty* (without ships, ports, roads and airports, etc., the ability to outsource is severely constrained)

Interestingly, the above factors happen to be inherent in an efficient capitalist system. So in a sense, 'platform companies' are the children of the capitalist system. They depend on the same pillars, and thrive on the same factors. Let us explain.

The history of capitalism is one of growth and progress; and where does capitalism find its growth? In two very strong forces:

1) **Growth can come from a rational organisation of talents**. David Ricardo gave the best expression of this source of growth in his law of comparative advantages. Even if a surgeon can type faster than his secretary, if cutting flesh is paid more by the hour than typing

letters, the surgeon should hire a secretary to do all of his typing, thereby freeing as much time as possible to cut flesh. This argument is of course most often applied to free trade (i.e., if France is good at producing wine and Senegal is good at producing world-class football players, then France should produce wine and Senegalese should play on the French football team ... or something like that).

2) **Growth can come from inventions put in place by entrepreneurs.** Growth triggered by inventions is a totally different kind of growth altogether. A new invention can trigger new demand, lead to new products, new management techniques and new markets. At the same time, inventions can also lead to the collapse of old products or old firms (e.g., with e-mail and fax machines, who still uses a telex?). This is the 'creative destruction' that Schumpeter described.

To promote the Ricardian kind of growth, one needs low trade barriers. To promote the Schumpeterian kind of growth, one needs low regulations, low taxes, easy access to capital and, most importantly, the ability and right to fail. These factors have been prevalent, at least across the Western world, for a generation. Are we about to change a good thing?

Intellectual giants, such as David Ricardo or Frederic Bastiat, have demonstrated so precisely all the advantages that accrue to countries engaged in free trade that one would think that the matter was settled once and for all. Unfortunately, protectionist rhetoric still rears its ugly head around the world every now and then.

Which, in a sense, is somewhat funny, for the free trade debate increasingly takes on Second Wave attributes. Take the Dell laptop on which these words are being typed. The keyboard was made in China, the PCB was made in Singapore and the motherboard was made in Malaysia. The flat screen was made in South Korea. The semis were made in Taiwan, on a US-owned design patent. Some of the software was compiled in the US, some in India, some in Sweden and some in Russia. The design of the notebook itself was done in Austin, Texas. Finally, the laptop was assembled in China. So where was the laptop 'made'? For the record, the label at the bottom of the notebook states 'Made in China' (which is ironic since, when we ordered it on the Dell website, we had to guarantee that this laptop would not be exported to, you guessed it, China!).

As the above Dell laptop example suggests, one of the greatest advantages of free trade is that countries become economically integrated with one another. This promotes both peace and faster economic growth. How does this work? Let us take a simple mathematical formula to express this.

A world with two centres has one line of communication linking the two points. The introduction of a third point creates two additional lines of communications. The emergence of a fourth pole brings the total to six and so forth. This enumeration could rapidly become tedious if mathematical theory did not offer a formula to explain this relationship: in a world with N centres, the number of links between the poles is $N(N-1)/2$. Excitingly, every day some new pole is added to the global economy: yesterday it was China. Today, it is India. Tomorrow, it could be Vietnam, the Ukraine, Egypt or Nigeria. Each time a new country joins the world economy, the number of lines of communication grows exponentially.

Let us suppose, as our Dell example suggests, that India, Russia and China are in the process of joining the rest of the world. Their addition requires massive capital spending increases in telecoms, airports, aircraft, harbours, ships, airline pilots, sailors and tourism capacity, etc.

To the effect of the number (N) of poles increasing, we must also add the fact that, as more people start to exchange ideas, more inventions come to surface. So not only do we witness an explosion in the number of lines of communication, but, all of a sudden, we witness the emergence of new means of communications. In time, this spurs growth further.

Events like the emergence of the fax, pagers, e-mail, mobile telephones and the Internet are obviously extremely important, and growth-inducing. Yet they are extremely difficult to model into econometric models or even classical economic analysis. It works as a step function, with strong periods of economic acceleration as new players and new means of communication emerge.

The bottom line, as Ricardo proved with his law of comparative advantages, is that each time a new country joins the table of world trade, everyone is enriched. Some are enriched more than others. But everyone is better off.

And when new ports, roads and airports are built, it gives the system a solid shot in the arm. Take the road improvements in India or China as an example. All of a sudden, regions, which in the past had been living hand to mouth, become open to the world. Food can move in lean times; workers can come in and out more easily, etc.

Free trade, combined with infrastructure spending, always leads to higher growth and higher standards of living. So with that in mind, we find the current attack on free trade from the US Congress (where the Central American Free Trade Agreement [CAFTA] only passed through with the slimmest of margins), the US presidency (which passed tariffs on steel imports and granted inordinately large domestic farm subsidies), the US Treasury (which keeps threatening action against China) and the European Union (which is stalling at the necessary opening-up to competition of European service industries, and banning Chinese textiles …) very worrying.

Yet, even if free trade is not as popular as it once was (one glance at a French newspaper will tell you as much), the recent US CAFTA vote highlights that, when push comes to shove, enough politicians will step away from the easy, grandstanding political rhetoric about saving jobs 'over here' against foreigners from 'over there'. This was also the message of the 2004 US election: protectionism does not win elections. In 2004, Senator Kerry railed against 'Benedict Arnold CEOs' and all that got him was a return ticket to the US Senate.

And it's the same thing in Europe. For all of his grandstanding against the 'Anglo-Saxon, ultra-liberal model' (liberal in French means capitalist), President Chirac has very little credibility in Europe's corridors of powers (where the man with the wind in his sails is the pro-free trade Tony Blair). Chirac also has shrinking amounts of credibility within his own party. Listen to what Patrick Devedjian, a minister under Chirac, had to say following the EMU Constitution referendum vote: 'the French model is not a model, since no-one wants to imitate it; it is not social, since it leads to record unemployment and it is not French, since it is founded on class struggle and a refusal of democracy'. He went on to add: 'ask yourselves why the CGT, the communist party and the FO don't want to see the model changed? Because it is their model! They are the authors of the so-called compromises, passed under the threat of strikes'.

With people like Mr Blair (or Mr Brown) and Mr Bush in power, the era of free trade is not yet over. As Mrs Merkel and Mr Sarkozy rise to power in the coming years (hopefully), Europe will hopefully evolve away from its 'Fortress Europe' mentality into a Europe ready to embrace the XXIst century. In short, the benefits of free trade have just started to accrue. We have seen nothing yet.

And the same could be said for technological progress.

As things stand, there are no physical limits whatsoever to the potential of creative destruction. And this for a simple reason: while the industrial revolution multiplied man's physical strength, the Internet revolution is multiplying man's intellectual strength. Resources that, until recently, had been locked away in the world's best libraries are now open for all to see – facts and figures that just ten years ago took dozens of hours to gather are now no further than a mouse-click away.

So at least three (free trade, infrastructure spending and technology) of the four pillars on which the 'platform company business model' rests feel fairly sturdy. But what about prevalent overcapacity? Fortunately, this too is an inherent part of capitalism.

Indeed, in the capitalist world, barring the emergence of monopolies, competition always leads to the most efficient producer lowering prices in order to drive his output higher. The fall in prices is therefore inherent in capitalism, which is why Marx believed capitalism sowed the seeds of its own destruction. A claim to which Bastiat would answer: in economics there is always what you see, and what you don't see. You see the fall in prices, but you do not see the rise in disposable income, or the increase in sales triggered by the falling prices.

This natural capitalist tendency was interrupted by the emergence of the social-democrat state, the nationalisation of a wide range of industries, and the Cold War of 1946-90. But it was the prevalent trend between 1820 and 1941.

It is once again prevalent today. Why? Because important parts of the world are clamouring to join the capitalist world, and in so doing, are using their excess savings (which are often large), to build excessive manufacturing capacity. Take the often-mentioned China market as an example.

In China today, one can reportedly find over 3,000 ball-bearing manufacturers (or over 300 car manufacturers, etc.). Unfortunately, the Chinese market is probably big enough for ten ball-bearing manufacturers. This means that 3,000 ball-bearing manufacturing company CEOs wake up every morning and wonder: 'how do I get to be one of the ten survivors?' In China, the answer to that question is simple enough: one gets to survive not by being the most profitable, or the most advanced technologically, or not even by being the best politically connected (though that helps). One gets to survive by being the biggest; by employing so many people that, when the down phase of the cycle occurs, the government can not afford to fire hundreds of thousands of workers. One becomes *'too big to fail'*.

This of course means that, when capital is offered up, all 3,000 ball-bearing manufacturers (following their 'too big to fail' business models) will grab it and spend it with both hands. Competing with each other for: 1) raw materials, 2) labour and 3) allocations on the overstretched power and transportation grids.

In previous cycles, Chinese manufacturers would in this way, end up with excess capacity that no-one would buy from them at any price (to use a technical term, the goods produced were 'crap').

Today, the situation is very different. After the recent Chinese capital-spending boom (Chinese capital spending has grown from 35% of GDP to 46% in the past five years), most Chinese manufacturers now produce goods that are competitive on the international market not only on price, but also on quality. This is a very important change, whose ramifications should become obvious in the coming year: China will work through the recent years of excess capital spending by exporting aggressively. Chinese goods will attempt to gain market share by undercutting any other producer out there.

This ability to undercut producers anywhere is obviously dependent on the ability of goods to move around. Indeed, as mentioned above, one of the important pillars of the 'platform company' business model is the ability to source production anywhere, and place producers in competition with one another.

Unfortunately, some events can severely disrupt this ability. And when that happens, the 'platform company' model is put to the test. Recent tests have included the dockers' strike on the US West Coast in the summer of 2001. The shutting down of the US air transportation grid following 9/11. The devastating impact of Katrina on the New Orleans port. All these events show that, in our Brave New World, a country's transport logistics grid is more important than ever before. So disruptions to it should be viewed with caution and weariness.

Given this last point, it is interesting to note that the Islamo-fascist terrorist against which we are struggling today seem far keener on disrupting our transportation grids then say, assassinating our political leaders (as their anarchist predecessors did in the early XXth century).

The US attacks of 11 September 2001 paralysed the domestic air transportation system, the Madrid attacks of 11 March 2003 took place on trains and the London 7 July 2005 attacks occurred on buses and subways. This determination to wreak havoc on our transportation systems could be based on an understanding that our infrastructure systems are the lynchpin of our 'brave new world'. If you manage to disrupt that, the damage you provoke can be much longer lasting than the killing of a politician who will be rapidly replaced.

Having said this, however we care to look at it, the pillars on which the 'platform company' model has been built appear to be solid foundations – at least in the short term. But what about the longer term? Is the excess capacity currently prevalent in the system not simply a cyclical phenomenon? And if so, aren't platform companies playing a dangerous game?

Clearing the "bubbles"

Looking back through recent History, we find that China, and Asia, have gone through several deflationary cycles; and the normal reaction has been to export the domestic deflationary pressures to the rest of the world (1994, 1998). Is the recurrence of this pattern a co-incidence? Or is it linked to the structure of production in China, Asia and around the world?

We believe it is the latter, and for a very simple reason: the only way one can get rid of overcapacities is to let the ownership of under performing assets move from 'weak hands', who are losing money on the assets, to 'strong hands', who can close down unproductive investments to start afresh. Without a rationalization of the structure of production, repetitive deflationary shocks are in the cards. To explain this further, let us take a step back, and review how bad investments are made in the first place.

Over the years, we have had the chance to witness several bubbles come and go. And, while it is obvious that two bubbles are never the same, it seems that bubbles often show similar patterns. In fact, we find two different kinds of bubbles. The first kind of bubble takes place on non-productive assets (typically land & real estate, but also tulips, or gold...). The second kind of bubble takes place on productive assets (canals, railroads, telecom lines). In the first kind of bubble, prices are bid higher due to a 'rarity' factor. In the second kind of bubble, prices rise because investors misjudge the future returns of the assets. When the bubbles burst, in the first case, we are left with no more land (or gold, or oil etc.) than what we started with. In the second case, productive capital has been put in place, which can still be exploited, either by its current owners, or by a new set of owners.

An example of the first kind of bubble would be the tulip-mania of 18th century Holland. An example of the second is the US and UK railway bubble of the 19th century or the telecom bubble of recent years. In Holland, when the tulip bubble burst, people were left with their eyes to cry with. In the US and the UK, when the railway bubble burst, the domestic economies still had trains to ride. All around the world, when the telecom bubble burst, consumers were left with the ability to make calls and transfer data more cheaply. In turn, this led to much higher levels of productivity (i.e. the birth of Indian and Philippino call centers), growth and a higher standard of living.

Another difference between bubbles is in the way that they are financed:

1– If the bubble is financed by banks, when the bubble bursts, the banks' capital disappears and the velocity of money collapses. (More on velocity later).

2– If the bubble is financed by capital markets (corporate bonds, junk bonds, and equities) those owning the overvalued assets take a beating. If they hold those assets on leverage, then the assets get transferred to more financially sound owners.

Otherwise, the buck stops with the overpriced assets' owners.

So the worst possible bubble (i.e. the most recessionary) is a bubble in unproductive assets (gold, land, tulips…) financed by banks. The best possible kind of bubble (i.e. one that does not hurt growth too badly) is a bubble in productive assets, financed by capital markets.

The Japanese bubble of the late 1980's was a 'bad' bubble. It was mostly in real estate and was financed by Japanese banks. By contrast, the US bubble of the late 1990's was a 'good' bubble. It was mostly in technology (too much telecom and computing expansion) and was financed by capital markets (junk bonds and equities).

But how do bubble burst?

As long as the return on invested capital is perceived to be higher than the cost of money, there is no problem in the system. However, there comes a time when the returns on investments fall below the cost of money. Sales start falling in the capital goods sector and/or in real estate. Needless to say, given the long delays, the momentum in the capital spending sector does not stop immediately and as such overcapacity is created.

Given that large proportions of investments have been financed by 'an inflation of debt', we run into a debt crisis. The creditors are alarmed and try to call their loans; as a result money supplies shrink. Banks go bankrupt. The price level goes down. The weight of the debt in real terms goes up faster than the repayments can be made. More bankruptcies follow. In such a world, happiness is a positive cash flow. In a supply-side cycle, the economy moves in three phases:

1) **The asset inflation (or debt inflation)** part of the cycle always takes place with the assertion that 'this time it is different', which for most of the period is true. In the upswing we always find two components: the belief in a new paradigm and the use of financial leverage. Indeed, the excess returns earned on assets acquired through leverage lead eventually to a massive increase in borrowing, and later on to overcapacity.

2) **The crisis** occurs when most of the market participants suddenly realize that the cost of money is now higher than the returns on capital. Usually the crisis is short. The chief result of the panic is to change massively the relative prices of assets between the 'new paradigm' sectors and the rest of the economy.

3) **The debt deflation** can then start: the cost of money moves even higher above the return on invested capital. The prices of assets

put as collateral on loans collapse. Bankruptcies and bank failures multiply. The money supplies contract. Prices fall across the board. Real interest rates go up, even if nominal interest rates fall, leading to more bankruptcies…

The end of the process takes place when the productive assets have moved from financially weak to financially strong owners. The rate of return on invested capital then moves above the interest rates (at a very low nominal level). And the next cycle can begin.

This last point is very important: for the deflation to end, **productive assets have to move from weak hands to strong hands.** But unfortunately, this does not happen so easily. For assets to move from weak hands to strong hands, one needs to have in place the following very important elements:

- A willingness from policy makers to allow companies to go bankrupt, regardless of the impact on local employment.

- Bankruptcy laws that permit creditors to gain control of under performing assets and restructure companies.

- Efficient markets which permit the transfers of under performing assets from weak hands to strong hands.

If the above factors are not in place, then inefficient companies continue to live on. They become 'zombie companies', waste capital (whether human or financial), drag down the returns on invested capital for competitors, maintain excess capacity in the system, and keep prices low for everyone.

Needless to say, none of the above necessary criteria for asset transfers are prevalent in China today. Or in Asia for that matter (note how long Japan's zombie companies were allowed to stick around). And even in Euroland, politicians do not like to see national champions fail. For instance while in recent years the UK government has allowed Rover, Marconi and others to hit the wall, the Italian government has stepped in to save Fiat, Alitalia etc. The French government twisted the French bank's arms to lend to Vivendi to avoid a bankruptcy etc.

All these differences might explain why Japan is still mired in a deflationary bust, while the US economy barely shrank as it adapted to a post-tech bubble world.

Fortunately for platform companies, it seems that most countries continue to be happy financing low return capital spending. And like parasites, the platform companies thrive on other people's excess capacity. Take China's capital spending bubble as an example:

So far, China's bubble has not really been on land and real estate prices are still decently low except for a few isolated pockets (i.e. Shanghai). The bubble has instead taken place in infrastructure spending (i.e. the world's fastest train links Shanghai to its brand new airport), factories (i.e. China has over 300 car manufacturers, 3000 ball bearing manufacturers) and construction.

China's capital spending has been financed mostly by one of three ways: retained earnings, foreign direct investment, or direct bank lending (or all at the same time). Which brings us to an important side point: in China, banks are not like banks in other countries. In China, banks are an extension of the government. Indeed, the way the system works in China is that, instead of granting a subsidy to a struggling steel producer in Manchuria, the government pressures a local bank into giving our struggling steel producer a loan. As a result, instead of having a debt to GDP ratio of 40% (or 105% like Italy, or 110% like Belgium), China's banks carry bad loans on their books equivalent to 40% of GDP.

The recent sharp increase in capital spending in China has not been financed by private lending institutions but by state-owned government banks. A big part of China's growth is occurring either directly on the government's balance sheets (i.e. spending by local authorities, towns and regions) or indirectly on the government's balance sheet (i.e. commercial banks). If/when the returns on capital fall below the cost of capital, we are unlikely to see a fire/sale of leveraged assets typical of a supply-side cycle deflationary bust; if for no other reason that a lot of the assets are on the government's book. In China the end-owner of all the 'weak assets' is the government; and the government is unlikely to become a 'forced seller'. In China, the government is the loser of first resort and it continues to maintain unproductive companies' existence.

This new reality means that we have witnessed an important transformation in the inflationary environments prevalent in our countries.

A discontinuous CPI

An old joke states that three econometricians go off shooting and spot a deer. The first shoots a foot to left. The second shoots a foot to the right. The third jumps up, shouting: 'we got him, we got him!'

To be sure, there is an element of approximation in both economics and econometrics. Take the $MV = PQ$ equation of Irving Fisher (which launched the field of econometrics). At any given point money supply (M) can rise but will that entail higher prices (P), or higher growth (Q)? And what if the private sector decides to sit on the cash (V) provided by the central banks?

Most economists today assume that increases and decreases in M (money supply) would impact Q (activity) first and foremost. The reason for this assumption is that, in every cycle between 1946 and 1990, this was mostly the case. But today, this assumption no longer makes sense: increasingly P is taking some of the cycle's adjustments. Since the early 1990s, at each deceleration in liquidity and economic growth, inflation has made lower lows; with each acceleration, inflation has made lower highs…

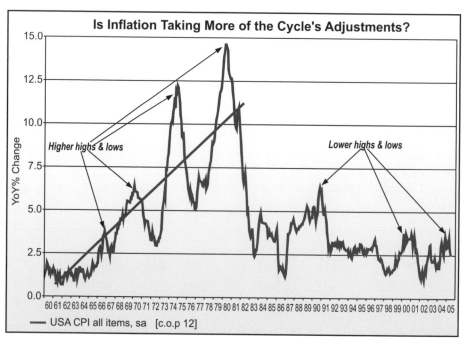

Until recently, we were living in a world of oligopolies. When average costs went up, so did average prices. But as the recent spike in oil, copper, transportation prices has shown, this is simply not the case any more. After all, who would have thought that the US$ could fall -35%, oil prices triple, copper prices triple, shipping rates triple and the US CPI would remain at, or under, 3%? Yet this is exactly what has happened in recent years. So, once again, we are forced to the conclusion that 'things are different this time'.

The difference is that, thanks to the combination of globalization, industry deregulation, technological progress, the spread of the Internet, and the emergence of the 'platform company model' (which feeds off all the above trends) we are moving towards a world with perfect information and perfect competition. In such a world, **prices are made at the margin, and no longer on average.**

The perfect examples of such pricing mechanisms can be found in the commodity markets where the information is, at the same time, available to most and widely spread. As we all know, commodity prices are far from stable: if there is a shortage of one barrel of oil, the price shoots up; if we have an overcapacity of one barrel, its price collapses. The same can be said of the freight rate for oil tankers, for copper, or for any well published price determined at the margin.

The combination of globalization and technology are helping platform companies such as Wal-Mart, Carrefour and others make a market for any good, product or service. And they can do this either directly through their purchasing units (Wal-Mart's computing facility is reportedly only second in the World to the Pentagon's) or using intermediaries specialized in such services, (Li & Fung, IDS Group, Linmark). Such companies know very rapidly if there is excess capacity somewhere and the price at which this extra capacity can be rented. In other words, platform companies engender an optimization, at the lowest possible price, of the global capacity of production.

Needless to say, the price of goods remains low only if there is excess capacity and the infrastructure is in place to move goods around. As soon as excess capacity disappears, then prices have to spike upwards to allocate efficiently again, this time the scarcity rather than the excess capacity.

In that respect, we all know that commodity prices move between feast and famine. If we apply the commodity model to the CPI then we can see that prices for all tradable goods in the CPI will remain under downward pressure, as long as there is a little overcapacity in each good. However, when we move into shortages, then prices will spike brutally up. Unfortunately this is very difficult to model.

Platform companies such as Wal-Mart are very much a 'dis-inflationary' force as they permit the optimization of the global producing economic base. In itself, this is a good thing. However, the question needs to be asked, what happens once this optimization has occurred? Does it lead to a rise in inflation? Fortunately, this question is not really of interest today, as the excess capacity of both labor and manufacturing capacity coming out of the Emerging Markets, and especially China, is absolutely massive.

Moreover, as long as saving rates across Asia remain high, then the cost of capital there will be inordinately low. And with a low cost of capital, companies will continue to follow their 'too big to fail' business models and over-invest. In other words, the future for platform companies, and for inflation, does not appear to be too cloudy.

In the past, price increases (oil, copper, labor…) meant a fall in consumer disposable income. Today, price increases lead to a fall in corporate profits for the companies that cannot increase productivity fast enough and who have, because of globalization and the internet, no pricing power. This explains why the rise in commodity prices witnessed in recent years has hurt neither the Western consumer, nor Western companies. Instead, the rise in commodity prices has killed the margins of Chinese companies.

This simple fact is visible in the dismal performance of Chinese equity markets. Despite the past five years impressive economic boom in China, and despite the fact that the overall population is today much wealthier than it was five years ago, Chinese stocks are trading at a five year low. Why? Simple enough: Chinese companies have been unable to make money in the boom. All their input costs have risen markedly, and, because of excess capacity in the system, Chinese companies have been unable to raise prices. The end result: shrinking margins and falling stock prices.

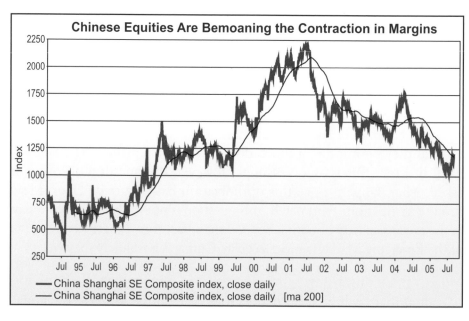

The 'platform company business model' has opened the way to a world in which inflation is now totally discontinuous. Inflation, instead of hurting the consumer, now wipes out the margins of the most marginal producer. And, as we will see later, this more marginal producer often tends to be 'over there' instead of 'close to home' (assuming, of course, that our reader is sitting somewhere in the Western World).

In any event, one thing we can surely agree on is that inflation today is, and feels, very different than inflation used to. In that respect 'things are different this time'. The difference is that capitalism is returning to its deflationary roots.

Why being rich keeps getting more expensive

The thing that is different this time, the bears would tell us, is that the inflation data is manipulated by central banks and Treasury officials to paint a much rosier picture than the underlying reality. They argue: 'How much has your cost of living risen in the past year?' To which most people answer 'an awful lot'.

Take a UK consumer as an example, Petrol prices are nearing £1 a litre and are 10% higher than last summer. Water, electricity and gas are up almost 15% on last year. Council taxes are soaring, private school fees and hospital charges are totally out of control, while taxis, hotels and restaurants seem to be much more expensive in London than in any other city in the world. Yet inflation, as measured by the official consumer price index, was just 2.3% in the year to July. While this was a marginally higher number than any recorded since 1997 on this particular index, 2.3% hardly amounts to an inflationary crisis and does not seem to reflect what many people feel about their own living costs.

Indeed, on the same day as the 2.3% inflation figure was published, the papers carried headlines not only about oil and petrol prices hitting new records, but also about prices reaching £100 a head in the best London restaurants, about air fares soaring and even about a new all-time high in art sales at Christies, which sold 178 works for over $1m in the first half of this year, compared with just 132 in the same period last year.

So what is really going on? Is concern about inflation really as passé as bell-bottom jeans? Or do the bear-bores have a point when they gripe about the extortionate cost of petrol or housing or school fees and murmur conspiratorially about government statisticians 'cheating' to disguise the stratospheric rise in the cost of living, which every fool can see with his own eyes?

The answer to these questions tells us a surprising amount about what is happening today not only in Britain but in the world economy as a whole. The fact is that the statisticians and bear bores are both right. The reasons for this paradox have nothing to do with statistical conspiracies in Britain, the US or elsewhere but a lot to do with the transformations our global economy is going through.

To see what we mean, consider the following figures. Over the past ten years the total cost of living in Britain, as measured by the official CPI, has risen by just 14%. But that very modest average increase has included inflation in some categories to make consumers wince: school fees, for example, are up 62%, hairdressing up 58%, holidays up 52% and eating-out up 33% on average, with top London restaurant prices showing much faster growth. Why then has the total cost of living remained so stable? Because the prices of mass-produced manufactured goods have been plunging: clothes prices down -42% in a decade, shoes are down -31% and consumer electronics are down -63%.

At its simplest, therefore, the disagreement over 'true' inflation simply reflects people's tendency to focus on prices that are rising and forget about the ones that are going down. But the extent and persistence of the divergence between service and goods prices in the past decade also suggests a less obvious and more important story in three parts.

The first part of this story relates to China's entry into the global economy and the emergence of the platform company model. By becoming the workshop of the world, China has pushed down the prices of all mass-produced manufactured goods. The virtually limitless supply of cheap labor and capital in China, and the chronic misallocations of capital, ensures that manufactured goods continue to get cheaper.

But the relentless downward pressure on manufactured prices from China has resulted in a second effect that is less widely understood, even among economists. Cheap imports from China have actually pushed up the prices of many goods and services which the Chinese cannot or do not produce - either because they lack the resources (oil) or the legal infrastructure (financial services) or simply because some things cannot be traded (housing and education).

People who see China purely as a source of downward pressure on prices forget that overall inflation in any economy is essentially determined by the availability of money. If monetary policy is successfully run (as it is in Britain or the US) to produce an overall inflation rate of 2-3%, while the prices of manufactured goods are persistently falling by 3 or 4%, prices elsewhere in the economy must rise faster to maintain the 2% average inflation rate. In this sense the ever-cheaper consumer goods from China have created more leeway for other prices in the world economy to go up. This effect has been particularly visible in the prices of goods and services which the Chinese are ravenously consuming but cannot produce themselves – for example oil, financial services and luxury property around the world.

Which brings us to the third, and most surprising, part of the inflation story. As the prices of financial services and luxury goods are driven persistently higher, service-producing countries such as Britain, Hong Kong or the US get richer relative to countries which specialize in manufacturing. And within those countries, the rich, who tend to work in high-end service industries which are relatively unaffected by competition from Asia, get richer still.

For the lucky bankers, lawyers and, yes, even economic analysts, who are benefiting from this seismic change in the structure of the global economy, there is, however, a sting in the tail. While we are getting richer, the high-end services, most obviously housing, travel and private education - on which many of us spend a disproportionate share of our incomes, are becoming more expensive, because of the very same global trends which are making us relatively rich.

That is why, even as inflation remains almost nonexistent, the talk in London and New York's bars and restaurants is of galloping prices. Being rich has never been so expensive. And staying rich is going to get more exorbitant by the day.

Should we therefore conclude that the trend towards globalization is locking lower classes into poverty and hardship? That Western countries will increasingly be split between the 'have' and the 'have not'? We do not think so. The platform company business model is having beneficial impacts across the whole economy, not just on prices.

Platform companies and the fall in economic volatility around the western world

As Western companies adopt the 'platform-company' model, and outsource the 'manufacturing' tasks, Western economies shed industrial jobs.

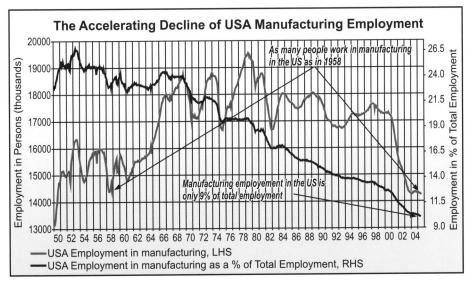

The Accelerating Decline of USA Manufacturing Employment

Countries like the US have lost so many industrial jobs in recent years (witness the drop between 2000 and 2004) that we should probably stop calling Western nations 'industrialized nations'. Western countries are increasingly anything but industrialized. Today, industry is in China, Poland, Korea, Mexico… Meanwhile economies like the US, the UK, the Netherlands should be called Western post-industrial nations, or Western Service economies…

Needless to say, the loss of industrial jobs is a disaster for industrial workers, and for politicians whose efforts depend on large pools of organized labor (more on that later). But unless one is an industrial worker, a trade union, or a left-wing democratic politician this is great news. Why? Because it means that the underlying economy loses most of its cyclicality. Let us explain:

- The industrial part of the production process is by far the most cyclical of the three step (design, produce, sell) process described in the first chapter.

- So as companies outsource the 'production' part, they effectively outsource the volatile part of the business process to someone else.

- This means that, when underlying economic activity is weaker then had been forecast, Western companies do not end up with the excess inventories, excess labor etc. It is the suppliers that have to deal with any excesses left over by the unforeseen economic soft spot.

To illustrate this, imagine the following situation. Due to an unexpected event (9/11? Tech bust? Very cold weather?) furniture sales in North America are all of a sudden much weaker than had been anticipated initially by IKEA. So what does IKEA do? It picks up the phone and calls its supplier in Indonesia (or Poland, Mexico etc.) and says:

Ikea: "Sorry. I know that, this time last year, we ordered 50,000 cupboards from you. But this month, we will only need 5,000."

Supplier: "But I have already bought the wood for 50,000 cupboards?"

Ikea: "Really? Then I guess you can give me a special deal on the 5,000 cupboards that I do need. After all, you will want to get rid of your wood inventory."

Supplier: "But how am I supposed to make my employee payrolls?"

Ikea: "Sorry my friend. There are two kinds of problem in the capitalist world in which we live: mine, and not mine. Your inventory and payroll issues are the second kind of problem."

Because of the slowdown in the demand for furniture, the supplier in Mexico (or elsewhere) is then forced to lay off people. Meanwhile, the designers at IKEA are hard at work on finding new designs that will draw people back into the stores, as are the IKEA marketing teams. In neither of the latter two activities do we witness many lay-offs. IKEA's people in Sweden and the United States remain duly employed and the shock is absorbed by the Mexican economy.

In a downturn, industrial workers always get the cull first. And as industrial workers are fired, their consumption falls, hereby forcing the next manufacturer to cut jobs etc. This is how we enter into a recessionary spiral. But now, industrial workers are abroad. Which means that, in a downturn, lay-offs are mild compared to previous cycles. As are the swings in overall economic activity.

To put it another way, when the Western economies were highly industrialized, the variable of adjustments for the economic cycle were either profits or employment; when the labor market was tight, companies would retain workers and take any adjustment on their bottom line and when the labor was loose, companies would try to maintain their profitability and fire workers. But today, with services gaining an ever important piece of the economic pie, the variable of adjustment for Western economies is no longer employment, or profits. It is imports.

Look at what has happened to US economic aggregates in recent years.

Firstly, the volatility of industrial production shrank as companies started to outsource the most volatile, or capital-intensive part of their production process.

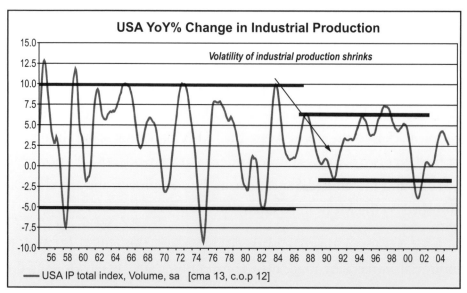

Secondly, as more and more workers held non-industrial jobs, the volatility of employment collapsed.

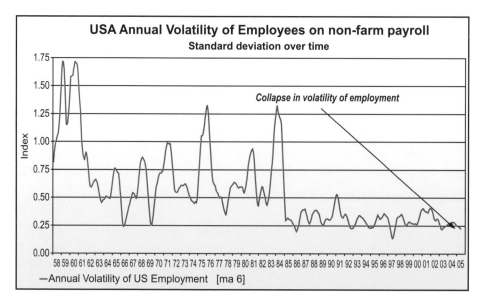

And finally, corporate profits increased, and their volatility fell.

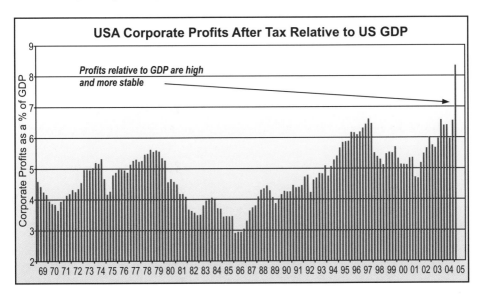

Meanwhile the volatility of US imports rose markedly.

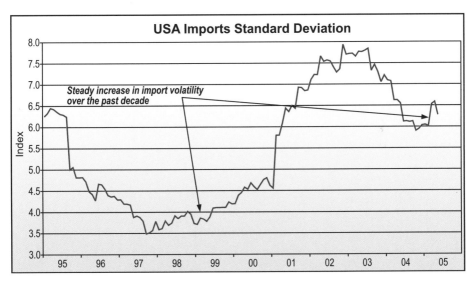

So when people claim that, today, all the US does is consume and never exports anything, this is not exactly true. Thanks to the platform companies, the US and other Western economies, (after all, IKEA is Swedish, Carrefour is French, Li & Fung is from Hong Kong etc.) have managed to export... the volatile part of their economic cycle!

A less volatile economic cycle is, needless to say, a great thing to have. It allows entrepreneurs to plan for the future more consistently, consumers to make decisions for the long term in the knowledge that they will not lose their jobs, governments to plan for fairly accurate tax receipts, companies to paint accurate pictures of future earnings to shareholders etc.

All this, of course, means that the fall in the volatility of the economic cycle has consequences of its own.

The world leverages up... but does it all make sense?

In 1985, Franco Modigliani won the Nobel Prize in economics for his work on how companies can optimize the leverage on their balance sheets, depending on the volatility of the economic cycle. Like all good economics, Modigliani's discovery made great intuitive sense: when the economic cycle is tame, companies can borrow more, and vice versa. Why? Because the problem with leverage is always the fear that, in lean times, one will not be able to make interest payments, and thereby go bust. But if now the 'lean times' aren't quite as lean as they used to be, then the ability to service debt, even at the trough of the economic cycle, is far greater.

And if this is true of companies, why should it be any different for individuals? Given the joint collapse in the volatility of the US economy and of US employment highlighted above, why shouldn't the US consumer borrow more and consume today instead of tomorrow? Indeed, historically, the problem with excessive leverage has been two fold:

a) Rising interest rates (if leverage was underwritten at variable, and not fixed rates).

b) The ability to service the debt when one lost his job.

Today, thanks to the emergence of the 'platform company' business model, the likelihood of losing one's job (if one is not an industrial worker) is much smaller than it used be. Consequently, the ability to service the debt at the trough of the cycle is less of an issue than it used to be.

This simple fact might help explain why, even in the midst of the 2001-2002 tech bust and recession, neither default rates or loan delinquencies really shot up. In any old economic cycle, an event such as 9/11 would have led to a major slowdown in economic activity, a rise in unemployment, a rise in delinquency rates etc. Instead, delinquency rates stayed close to record lows (and have fallen more since then).

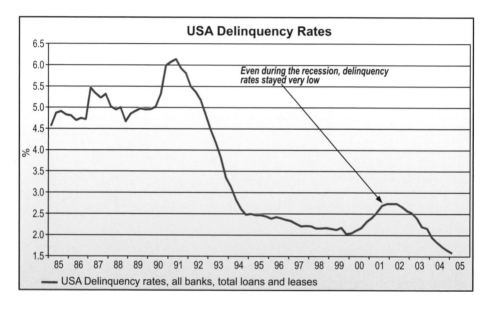

Surely this is an important message.

Looking at the continued fall of US delinquency rates, one is forced to conclude that something is different this time. And what is different is the nature of the job of the average American worker. One generation ago, the average American worker was a blue-collar industrial male. Today, there is no such thing as the average worker. He can be a she; which means that, increasingly, two people cover a mortgage – a fact which also helps reduce the likelihood of defaults. And he or she usually works in a service post far less dependent on the vagaries of the economic cycle than his or her father did.

Today, when US economic activity turns south, the US consumer, despite his 'over-leveraged' status, of concern to so many, continues to power ahead. In recent years, the US consumer has remained the bedrock of the world economy because he did not lose his job; nor did he worry about the possibility that he might lose his job.

This confidence in his employment outlook allows the US consumer to leverage up, even in lean economic times. With the fall in the volatility of the US economic cycle, the propensity of American consumers to leverage up in order to buy consumer goods, automobiles or real estate has risen markedly. This makes perfect economic sense. As Modigliani showed, less volatility equals more debt.

Yet, instead of focusing on the left part of the equation (less volatility in the economic cycle), most economists prefer to focus on the right part of the equation (more consumer debt). From there, they draw nightmare scenarios, talk of un-sustainability etc. But they are missing the forest for the trees; for without volatility in the economic cycle, especially in employment, the American consumer's propensity to leverage up is not as foolish, or reckless, as might appear at first glance.

Does what makes sense for the US consumer also make sense for the consumer elsewhere? Undeniably, as the world's lone super-power, the US is usually an important trendsetter. This is especially true for financial products. Who had heard of venture capital funds, junk bonds, LBOs, before those products where invented in the US? So, as the US invents various consumer credit tools (securitization of mortgages, credit card debt etc.), should we be surprised to see these products appear all around the World?

For some countries (the UK, Australia, Sweden), the leveraging of the consumer makes perfect sense. The underlying economies are going through the same transformation, and the same fall in volatility, as the US economy. In fact, countries like the UK or the Netherlands are as much, 'platform company' economies as the US and maybe even more so. So why shouldn't the consumer there leverage up as well?

The leveraging of the Western consumer makes all the more sense when one considers that the Western consumer is today in an historically unprecedented place. The average Western consumer is able to call on a pool of capital larger than ever. And this is for a simple reason: for over sixty years, the pool of available capital has not been destroyed by a major War (i.e. WWI, WWII) or a tragic natural disaster (i.e. the Great Kanto Earthquake of 1923 which leveled Tokyo). As a consequence, the current generation of Western twenty and thirty somethings is the first to be able to draw on the savings of parents / grand-parents etc.

Of course, this 'ample liquidity environment' can change rapidly. For example, the destruction of New Orleans by Hurricane Katrina will be a severe economic blow for the entire Gulf Coast region for years to come. The liquidity drain on the global economic system will likely add up to hundreds of billions of US$.

But there is another element to the 'ample liquidity environment', namely that in the rich, Western world, there are increasingly less 'kids' and more adults. And this is for a simple reason: the children of the baby boom generations did not keep up the hard reproducing work of their forefathers. So kids can easily hit-up parents for money... and they no longer need to share the parental loot with numerous brothers and sisters. The western world's demographic changes are having a major impact on the availability of capital.

One generation ago, twenty five year olds did not buy apartments. Today, it is a frequent event made possible by the fact that:

a) Twenty five year olds can draw on their parents' savings in a way that their parents could not draw on their own parents' savings.

b) Twenty five year olds have a good visibility of their future earning power.

Is the fact that twenty five year olds are buying apartments in record numbers to be bemoaned or cherished? Reading *The Economist*, you would think it was a negative development.

Unfortunately, the same trends are not prevalent in Emerging Markets. Emerging Market consumers who borrow, have to do so solely on the basis of their future cash-flows; not against any assets that they, or their parents, might hold. Which raises an important quandary.

In the chapters above, we have argued that the volatility of the US economy is contracting because US companies are increasingly sending the low-value added, high fixed costs, part of their production process abroad. But if the US is exporting its volatility, it means that someone is importing it. This someone is usually in an 'emerging market' (China, Mexico, Brazil, South Korea…).

In turn, this means that, while the US worker is less likely to be fired at the bottom of the cycle (which allows him to take on more leverage), the Emerging Market consumer is more likely to get fired when times get lean (as illustrated in the above IKEA-Mexican producer example). Which means that, while the income of the Emerging Market consumer is rising fast, so is the volatility of that income.

Looking at the history of commercial banks, we know that commercial banks like to get into businesses at the top. And today, the main common point seems to be a desire to increase exposure to the Emerging Market consumer, especially in China. In recent months, Goldman Sachs, American Express, Allianz, Credit Agricole, Royal Bank of Scotland, BNP Paribas, Bank of America, Temasek, Merrill Lynch have all announced plans to buy stakes in China's big banks (whether Agricultural Bank of China, ICBC, CCB or BoC). And the justification was usually always the same: to gain access to the rapidly growing Chinese consumer.

But does this make sense? In essence, Western banks can lend either to:

a) The Western consumer: strong asset base, low volatility of cash flows

b) The Emerging Market consumer: no asset base, high volatility of cash flows

Undeniably, the Emerging Market consumer option has the wind in his sails: it offers higher fees, and has a much stronger growth potential. It is a business that commercial banks should go after.

But at the trough of the cycle, it might prove to be a far more 'cyclical' than 'structural' business than some managements have anticipated. Building big consumer lending businesses in emerging markets will likely lead to higher profits, but it might also lead to a greater volatility in those profits. And will shareholders reward this higher, more volatile, growth with higher multiples?

The irresistible rise of real estate

As suggested above, more often than not, the increase in leverage ends up financing real estate purchases; and this, the bears tell us, is paving the way for a disaster. They argue that, given the fact that real estate is in a 'bubble', tacking leverage onto it is putting our financial system on the brink of a systemic risk. Once real estate collapses, we will face an 'ice age'. Fortunately, for all the talk of 'ice-ages', the down jackets can probably remain in the closets. Indeed, it seems that the argument that real estate is in a 'bubble' fails to take into account some of the economic transformations mentioned above.

The first economic transformation is the rise in consumer disposable income, especially at the high end, which is a direct consequence of globalization (see Chapter 5). As the goods consumers buy keep falling in price, the average consumer is left with more money in his pocket; and where does he spend this money? More often than not, on his house.

This rise in disposable income might help explain why US house prices have risen 3.5x since 1980 (an average annual growth rate of 5%, against an average annual growth rate of 6% for US nominal GDP). As goods get cheaper, houses become more expensive. What we are facing is not a bubble, but an impressive change in relative pricing. An anecdote illustrates this point. In 1981, when Charles moved to London, one of his clients was proud of the fact that, for the first time ever, his London apartment was finally worth more than his car. Who could say that today with a straight face?

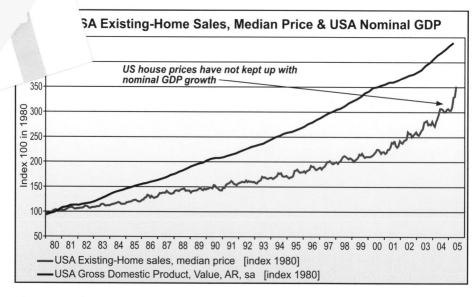

USA Existing-Home Sales, Median Price & USA Nominal GDP

US house prices have not kept up with nominal GDP growth

Index 100 in 1980

— USA Existing-Home sales, median price [index 1980]
— USA Gross Domestic Product, Value, AR, sa [index 1980]

The second transformation, as seen in Chapter 6, is that the US economy, and employment, are far less volatile than they used to be. This means that the average worker today is less likely to get fired at the bottom of the economic cycle, and has more visibility as to his future earnings power. In turn, this means that it makes economic sense for him a) to borrow more and b) for the bank to lend to him increasing amounts of money.

A third important change is linked to the structure of the workforce. In the old days, household income was usually dependent on just one person (the working man). Now, more often than not, there are two people (husband and wife) working in every household. This also makes the average household income far less volatile than in the past; which means that comparing today's household income with yesterday's (as the doom-mongers are wont to do) is akin to comparing apples and oranges.

A final and very important change has been the collapse in inflation and, with it, the collapse in long-term interest rates. At the end of the day, one of the main drivers of a real estate market anywhere is the propensity of the population to service their mortgages. And the propensity to service mortgages has risen in recent years thanks to the continued low interest rates.

For all the constant talk about the forthcoming collapse of US real estate, it is hard to see what the trigger will be for a sudden fall in prices. To get a true collapse in real estate prices you either need prices to get to truly stupid levels (i.e. Tokyo in 1989, Hong Kong in 1997) and/or a serious increase in bank foreclosures. Indeed, only when banks 'get the keys' and become desperate sellers do we usually see prices collapse. With this last point in mind, we have a hard time envisaging a rise in US foreclosures given that a) unemployment is low and falling, b) disposable income is still rising and c) mortgage rates are low and falling.

The recent experiences of the UK and Australian real estate markets (two economies very similar to the US) should also warrant caution on excessive bearishness on US real estate. Indeed:

a) By any measure, UK and Australian real estate are far more overvalued than real estate in the US;

b) The Australian & UK central banks tightened earlier and more aggressively than the Fed;

c) The Australian and UK real estate markets are far more interest rate sensitive than the US real estate market (most people have adjustable rate mortgages);

d) UK and Australian consumers are at least as leveraged, if not more, than the US consumer;

e) The UK & Australian economies have slowed more than the US in recent months...

And yet, despite all of the above, and despite widespread belief that those markets would crumble (belief in which we shared; Charles sold his London house in June '04), UK & Australian real estate have held up very decently. So why should the US real estate market be any different?

But here, once again, there is 'what we see', the impressive rise in house prices, and 'what we don't see'. The 'what we don't see' includes the sustained fall in interest rates, the rise in disposable incomes across the Western World, the new methods of real estate financing, the fall in the volatility of consumer earnings etc. Any of these individually could explain the rise in real estate. Together, they are a very potent force, which should not be discounted lightly.

Let us return to the fall in interest rates. We can all agree that houses are very long duration assets. In fact, they are probably the longest duration asset out there; the tower in Charles' Provence house was built in the XIVth century and is still standing strong.

Long duration assets tend to be far more sensitive to changes in interest rates than short duration assets. Take a 30 year Freddie Mac mortgage bond as an example: in 1982, the bond was yielding 18.45% and the price of a thirty year mortgage zero coupon bond was 6.22. Today, with yields at 5.58%, the price of the same thirty-year zero coupon is 19.81.

Which leads us to the following question: since housing is, by definition, a very long duration asset, and given all the talk about overvalued houses, and bubble like conditions in real estate, have house prices in the US gone up more-or less– than the price of a 30 year mortgage zero coupon? Indexing the prices of both at 100 ten years ago, we come up with this:

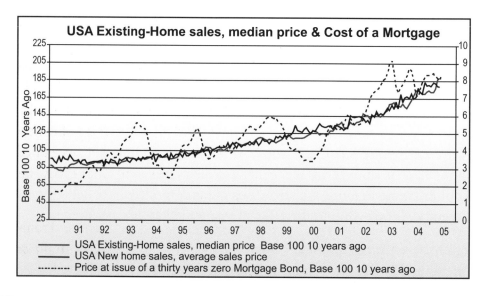

The result is obvious: House prices, whether median or average, have adjusted dollar for dollar for the decline in long rates, but nothing more. In other words, two assets of similar long-term duration have had the same price increases. Interestingly, we come up with the same result for the UK. Since 1982, house prices in the UK have gone up exactly as much as the price at issue, of a thirty year zero coupon UK government bond.

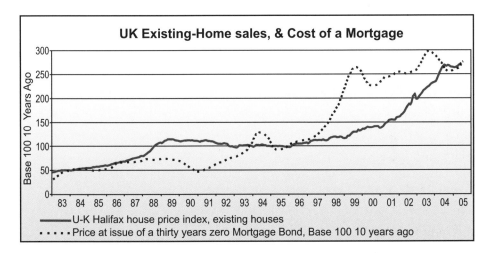

Thanks to 'platform companies', capital today is more efficiently allocated and used than in the past. As a result, we have witnessed a once in a lifetime decline in long interest rates. This decline in long interest rates has a huge impact on long duration assets. And which is the most widely held long duration asset in the world? Houses in countries where the rule of law prevails. In other words, for all the talk of an unsustainable bubble in real estate, all we have witnessed in the past decade is a movement by house prices around the world to price themselves according to the new cost of money. There is nothing bubble-like in such a move, except of course if long rates were to go up savagely from now on. As of today, we see no evidence whatsoever of a spike in long rates.

Once again, things are different this time. This means that the doom-mongers might have to wait longer for the collapse in UK, Australia & US real estate than they imagined possible.

Consumption - economists vs accountants

But then, of course, most dismal scientists would tell us that a situation in which the Western world consumes, through increasing leverage, while Emerging Markets (especially Asia) produce, is not 'sustainable'. In fact, we are told that the large US trade deficits (which result from this new 'platform company' business organization) will one day lead to a 'US$ crisis'; a refusal by foreigners to finance US consumption etc.

To illustrate what is wrong with economists' view the world, and how the above view has little resemblance to reality, consider the following example: Let us assume that a Dell PC sells in the US for US$700. Now let's have a look at how this very simple transaction is recorded in a) Accounting 101 and in b) Economics 101.

Accounting 101:
The flat screen, built in Taiwan, costs US$300. The margin of the Taiwanese manufacturer is US$30. The mechanical part and the box, built in China, cost US$100, with a margin of US$5. The Intel chip (designed in the US but made by TSMC in Taiwan) cost US$70 with a margin of US$35 going back to Intel and US$5 going to TSMC. The Microsoft software cost US$200, with a margin of 90%, or US$180. Dell tacks on a US$30 profit for selling the PC.

Profits for the US economy: US$35 (Intel) + US$180 (MSFT) + US$30 (Dell) = US$245
Profits for foreign economies: US$30 (Taiwanese flat screen maker) + US$5 (TSMC) + US$5 (Chinese assembly line) = US$40
Difference: + US$205 on behalf of US companies

Conclusion: this looks like a good deal all around for the US: the US consumer gets a cheap PC and US companies capture most of the profits in the process. On an accounting basis, everything looks rosy…

Now let's see how an economist views the above transactions.

Economics 101:
Imports: US$470 (price of the PC minus the Dell mark-up and Microsoft software); Exports: US$0
Trade Deficit= US$470.
Increase in GDP, due to Microsoft, Dell and Intel profits = US$245
Net loss for the US economy, US$ 470-US$245 = -US$225

Conclusion drawn by the economists: this is a really unsustainable situation. The US economy is moving more and more in debt to foreigners who one day could decide not to sell in the US anymore, leading to a collapse in the US$, a rise in US interest rates, etc.

But in the real world, is this situation really unsustainable? Absolutely not!

What is unsustainable is measuring global trade flows in terms of sales, without looking at profits - which is what trade numbers do – and deriving investment implications from these measures. If the fellows exporting to the US make on average a margin of 1%, while US exporters churn out margins of 20%, then which economy would you rather own?

In a world in which platform companies are becoming increasingly important, the so-called distortions will only continue to grow. Indeed, Dell will continue to outsource PC production & assembly to the cheapest manufacturer, who will most likely be working on razor thin margins; but meanwhile, Dell's profits will continue to rise.

Economists assume that, over time, imports and exports have to balance, otherwise a country moves into debt. And then, one day the music stops and 'it is time to pay up!' This simple, Calvinist idea would be true if margins on imports and margins on exports were the same, but this is simply never the case. And it is increasingly less so; if anything, margins have been diverging, not converging.

In Anglo-Saxon Countries, we find high margins, low sales, extremely low volatility of unemployment and of production. As a result, domestic workers have a very stable income, on which they can put a fair amount of debt (the optimum debt is very high since jobs are very stable – see above). The prevalent macro-conditions mean that the urge to save aggressively is nonexistent, and that the savings ratio is low. Domestic companies have a positive cash flow and a very high ROIC, so the probability of them going bankrupt is almost zero (except through fraud, or massive mismanagement). The need for large amounts of precautionary capital is therefore also very low.

In Emerging Markets, we find low margins, high sales, extremely high volatility of employment and production. As a result, domestic workers have a very unstable income, on which they can put little debt (see above). Domestic companies tend to work with low ROIC, and negative cash-flows all the time, so they must accumulate a huge amount of precautionary savings (large shareholder equity), should a liquidity crisis occur. The domestic saving ratios need to be very high.

Trade balances are computed on sales. Implicit in this computation are two hypotheses:

a) That the margins on imports and exports are the same and

b) That sales must balance each other over the long term.

As noted above, the first assumption makes no economic sense whatsoever. And the second is also way off the mark.

Indeed, instead of having sales balance off each other over the long term, goods can be exchanged for assets. So the so-called 'US debt to the outside world' can be easily repaid by the sale of US assets to foreigners. And this does not mean that the US gets poorer over time (i.e. the share-cropper society of Mr Buffett), unless of course one wants to assume that the stock of US assets is fixed and does not grow over time (a silly assumption to make).

Consider the following: companies in the US have very stable and robust earnings. In the previous example, US companies had profits of US$245/US$700. Now let us imagine that, in the stock market, these earnings are capitalised at 20x on average. This gives a market cap of US$4,900 per computer sold. And then we get to the all important question: will the Chinese/Taiwanese savers (who sold a PC to the US and so received US$) prefer to buy the assets of their own country? Or those of the United States? Obviously, everything depends on relative prices; but at equal price, the Chinese savers will want to be invested in the 'safer' US assets (if given the choice).

Assuming that, in China/Taiwan, salaries represent 50% of sales or US$220, and that the poor factory workers save 50% of their salaries, then the employees can buy US$110 worth of high quality shares in the US, or US$110/US$4,900=2.2%.

If the demand for computers in the US increases by 10%, then the trade deficit will become even bigger, but the poor Chinese worker will still only be able to buy 2.2% of US equities with his gains (since the price of US assets will also rise by 10%). The poor Chinese worker will be chasing a moving target.

Let's leave theory behind and return to the real world. In 1991, foreigners owned 11% of the US stock market. Since 1991, the US stock market (dividend included) has quadrupled. Today, after a continued deterioration in the US current account deficit, foreigners own 17% of the US market.

The fact that foreigners increased their holdings in the last 14 years by 50% goes a long way in explaining why the US stock market has quadrupled (since prices are made at the margin). But, at the end of the day, everybody is richer: the US consumer, the owners of US companies, the Chinese companies and the Chinese workers. And as long as the US has assets to sell, then there will be no reason to worry.

The US has a trade deficit with China (or Taiwan, or Korea...) not because China has a comparative advantage, but because the US has a perfect knowledge of where to domicile production at the lowest possible cost. And this is a very important differentiation. Today, the comparative advantage is with the US; and, because manufacturing is a low value-added, highly cyclical, low return on investment activity, the US runs a very high trade deficit in manufactured goods (which, unlike services, are easy to count when they come in and out of the country). But this deficit is compensated by a colossal rise in corporate earnings.

Funnily enough, most economists seem to believe that a comparative advantage should always lead to a trade surplus. It does not. A comparative advantage leads to a higher standard of living. Which is what we have witnessed in the US. So this deficit is viable as long as corporate profits rise more than the current account deficit deteriorates, and as long as asset prices acknowledge this increase. This is exactly what has happened in the US.

In the past five years, US profits (cash-flows) have increased by US$500 billion and the US trade deficit has increased by US$250 billion. Assuming that the assets generating the profits are selling at 20x earnings, this leads to an increase in US assets of US$ 10,000 billion, to be compared with a deterioration in the external debt situation of less than US$1,200 billion. Where is the lack of sustainability?

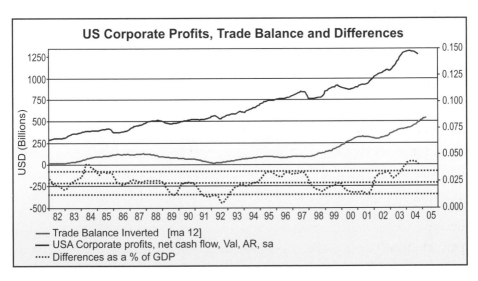

US Corporate Profits, Trade Balance and Differences

— Trade Balance Inverted [ma 12]
— USA Corporate profits, net cash flow, Val, AR, sa
····· Differences as a % of GDP

The bears will nevertheless question how long the US can afford to run a current account deficit of US$700 billion or 5.7% of America's $12.2 trillion GDP. Our answer: much longer than implied by bogus comparisons of deficits with GDP.

Comparisons with GDP are commonly used as an index of current account sustainability, but this does not make them right. Since the current account is the counterpart of a capital inflow, sustainability depends not on the US economy's annual output, but on how much US capital foreigners are willing, or able, to acquire. Since foreigners are always keen to buy US assets at a price (not only because the US$ is the world's reserve currency but also because owning property in America is the ultimate safety for every rich family in every country around the world), the real limit on the US current account is set by the amount of their country that Americans are prepared to sell.

Once this is understood, it becomes clear that the current account should be compared not with GDP but with the value of US assets.

The Fed's latest valuation puts US private net assets at US$49 trillion. This figure, which includes the net equity value of US private businesses and corporations and allows for all foreign and domestic debts, but excludes both assets and liabilities of the government, represents a reasonable estimate of America's total net assets (since the government's $5 trillion in liabilities and assets roughly net out). The annual capital inflow required to finance a $700 billion trade deficit represents just 1.4% of this total. Given that net private assets have been growing at a steady 6% each year since the start of the present decade, the trade deficit pre-empts less than one-quarter of this increase in wealth.

The conclusion is clear: if America's wealth keeps growing about as fast as it has in the past decade (and we have no reason to believe that it will not), the current account will remain sustainable, whether it stays at $700 billion, falls to $500 billion or soars to $1 trillion a year.

The US sits on top of an economic system whereas:

a) The US consumer buys Chinese made goods for very little money and on which the Chinese producer makes no margin.

b) The Chinese then take their hard earned US$ and buy overpriced US assets (whether US Treasury bills, the IBM PC Unit, etc.)

Why should we be worried about someone who sells overvalued assets and buys undervalued goods? It seems smarter than doing the opposite. It would make more sense to be worried about the guy who sells undervalued goods to buy overvalued assets (i.e. China).

The fact that the US consumer has a lot of debt on his balance sheet goes without saying. Not that this keeps a number of financial commentators and publications from saying it over and over again and then again some more. However, all of those who have made it their business over recent years (decades?) to predict the forthcoming demise of the US consumer because of his level of debt have been disappointed. So what has gone wrong for the US perma-bears? Is it just a question of timing? Or are we facing a new economic cycle where the adjustments forced onto the Western consumer are much milder and the US consumer is therefore able to withstand a much higher debt load? Recent events point to the latter.

In the old US economic cycle, the sequence of events was roughly as follows:

Industrial production would slow; the Fed would ease; short rates and long rates would fall; housing would pick up (thanks to the low rates) along with consumption; unemployment would start to fall; economic activity would accelerate; companies would start to invest; the trade deficit would deteriorate; the US$ would weaken; inflation would bottom out and start to rise; the Fed would then tighten; liquidity would shrink; the US$ would rise; industrial production would slow and ...go back to the beginning...

However, if the ideas developed on the previous pages are right, then the above cycle (with which investors are familiar) should be replaced by a new economic cycle. And this cycle should work as such:

A bust occurs because of a massive misallocation of capital somewhere in the system (i.e. Asian crisis, TMT crash…), this leads to a fall in prices in the US (as platform companies take advantage of the excess capacity and import cheap goods); the Fed cuts rates; US consumers' disposable incomes rise (thanks to lower prices and lower interest payments); consumption booms; the US trade deficit deteriorates massively; the US$ falls…. (So far, so very familiar).

But then inflation remains low as platform companies simply start to source their purchases in countries that have not revalued against the dollar (i.e. China, Malaysia) or even devalued (Mexico). The Fed continues to maintain artificially low interest rates, housing booms, and so does consumption. The bears warn us again that it will all end in tears.

The US$ then falls further. This leads to a great increase in liquidity outside of the US and central bank reserves go through the roof. Housing, stock markets and production (outside of the US) boom. At this stage, wealth in enormous amount is created both in, and out, of the US. Inflation remains low, the US$ keeps falling, the bears…(see above).

However, at some point, US assets in the eyes of foreigners become incredibly cheap. Then the industrialists who have made money selling to platform companies decide that having part of their assets in the US makes sense on a risk adjusted basis. They start buying real estate in Miami, or in New York. They no longer remit their excess US$ to their central banks, but instead use them to bid up US assets. The growth of foreign central bank reserves held at the Fed starts to decelerate. The US$ starts to rise, regardless of what the US current account deficit does. Liquidity outside of the US shrinks since the foreign private sector is recycling its earned US$ back into the US (instead of forcing their central bank to print money). This leads to a global liquidity crunch and the marginal players go bust. Platform companies then come in and tighten the screws on their suppliers.

This is the phase of the cycle in which platform companies clean up.

In the Second Wave world, countries had to exchange gold to settle a negative current. Today, instead of having to keep around an unproductive asset in bank vaults for the single purpose of settling deficits countries can instead sell some of their domestic assets (real estate, farm land, shares, bonds…).

The exchange standard of the Second Wave world was built around gold. This collapsed in 1972 under the weight of its own contradictions.

The exchange standard of the Third Wave world is built around assets. And everyone is richer for it for, unlike gold, there are no limits to the growth of assets.

But aren't all the good jobs being shipped abroad?

We are always surprised by how many economists and analysts refuse to look at the world through Ricardian or Schumpeterian lenses, and instead take a Malthusian approach to most problems; presenting arguments of 'there won't be enough for everybody'. The Malthusian stance is all the more surprising since it has been discredited time and again. Indeed, Malthus' prediction of wars and famines because of the divergence between the geometric growth in population and the arithmetic growth in food production, was off the mark nearly as soon as he formulated it. Western Europe witnessed one more large famine (the potato famine in Ireland) and never went hungry again (except during wars). Same with the Club of Rome's late 1970s ideas that we would run out of energy, metals etc. Each time economists have feared that there 'won't be enough for everyone', they have usually soon found out that the one thing there is always plenty of is humble pie.

Why do we bring this up? Because the most common stance amongst the bears, when presented with the above arguments, is to argue that, with globalization, 'all the good jobs are being shipped abroad'. So we are building a 'financial house of cards on very weak foundations'. Take our very good friend Marc Faber in his August 2005 *Gloom Boom Doom Report*. Marc states: *'I am fully aware that some observers* (maybe GaveKal?) *will argue that it doesn't matter that US companies are increasingly moving their own plants overseas, or outsourcing altogether, because the improved profits that result from the outsourcing accrue to the parent company... However, what about the long term? How beneficial is it going to be for Western industrialized companies if IBM were to lay off 13,000 people over the next twelve months in the US and hire 14,000 in India… I suppose even a non-economist could see that the movement offshore of sophisticated manufacturing and well-paid service jobs has to have some negative macro-economic consequences…'*

The Malthusian argument that there are only so many 'good jobs' strikes us as both odd and dangerous.

It is odd because we frankly do not understand the need to antagonize 'profits' against 'the long term'. As Adam Smith adequately proved, the capitalist system works over the long term for the very reason that every single participant in the market place aims to maximize his profit. Once agents start to act in the market for reasons other than profits, that's usually when things start to go astray.

The fact that, thanks to thanks to globalization, outsourcing, and the adoption of the platform company model, US corporate profits keep making record highs should not be bemoaned; it is excellent news, not only for the 60% of Americans who own shares (whether directly or through their pension plans) but for the greater society at large.

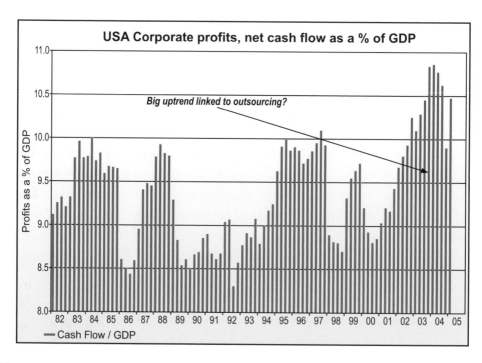

Of course, a Marxist would argue that the constant rise of corporate profits as a % of GDP is not a good thing at all. It shows that 'capital' is reaping all the rewards while 'labor' is getting the sharp end of the stick.

Needless to say, we do not buy the Marxist argument for a second. For a start, any kind of debate based on the premise that paid labor is inherently a form of capitalist exploitation, which alienates the worker from his true humanity, is a sad reflection of 'second wave' thinking. In our new Toffleresque 'third wave world of prosumers', a dichotomy between labor and capital is increasingly less relevant. As mentioned above, 60% of Americans own shares... So are they oppressed workers? Or evil capitalists? In our new world, the shareholders and the workers are increasingly one and the same. The Marxist, second-wave, thinking which still suffuses political and economic thinking in large parts of Europe and academia and presents employment as an essentially adversarial relationship between capital and labor has, little intellectual credit. It simply does not reflect current economic realities. The market economy is simply not a class battlefield, but is instead a mutually beneficial enterprise. Opposing 'profits and capital' to 'labor' really makes no sense at all in a world where a company's assets increasingly ride the elevator every morning and evening.

This impression is further confirmed by a recent Pew Global Attitudes survey, which showed that 41% of Britons and 44% of Americans describe themselves as 'very satisfied' with their employment, compared with only 24% of the French. The survey also showed that Britons and Americans were more satisfied with their general lifestyle and far more optimistic about the future than the French. Isn't it ironic that, in the country where the workers are the most protected against the 'excesses of capital', the workers happen to also be the most miserable? (And for those tempted to say it, this divergence does not come from the fact that French people are grumpier!)

In essence, as the platform company model has taken root in the UK and the US economies, workers in those two countries have traded in tamer wage growth relative to profit growth in the ascending phase of the cycle against higher job security (volatility of unemployment has collapsed). To us, this seems to be a good trade. Especially as along with the higher job security has come a steady rise in employment:

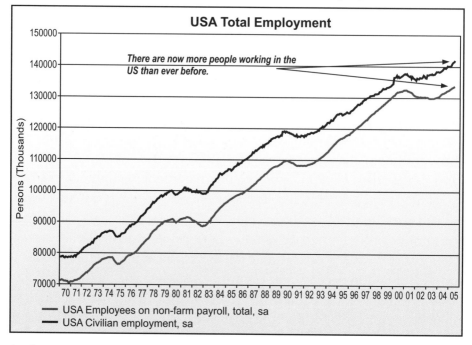

And a sustained rise in disposable income:

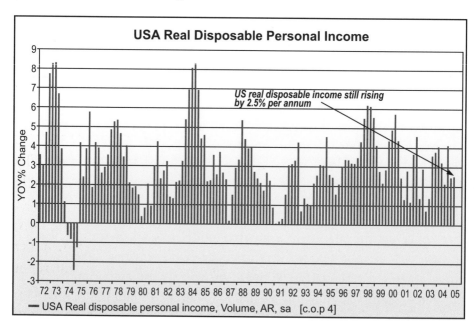

Of course, the bears will then tell us that the above numbers are meaningless since:

a) They are given by the Fed, which has an incentive to manipulate and deceive investors and

b) The rise in jobs is in 'precarious jobs'. While the US consumer is forced (still in our friend Marc's words) to become a *'real estate agent, stock-broker, croupier, hedge fund manager, or Washington lobbyist'*, with all the good IBM or Boeing jobs being sent abroad.

That last comment is undeniably true: in the past thirty years, the percentage of blue collar workers in the US economy has collapsed:

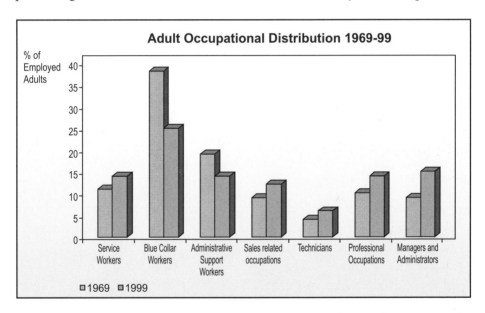

But why should this be a disaster, or even an event that we bemoan? Why would working as a sales clerk be worse than working on an assembly line? If one is not wearing a hard hat, and bringing a lunch-box into work, is one not really working? Listening to a number of economists, one gets the feeling that, if one is not clocking-in, wearing a wife-beater and sweating profusely over the course of a hard day's work, one is not really contributing to society; instead one is a mere parasite, a paper-pusher living off other people's labor. But is this not a Second-Wave way of looking at our Third-Wave world? Just like the physiocrats, who with their First Wave thinking totally missed the industrial revolution unfolding in their front of their eyes, are economists today not missing the Third Wave revolution going on around us simply because they are focusing on Second-Wave Marxist metrics? We believe they are.

In the Third Wave economy described by Toffler, the source of all wealth is knowledge. Working on the assembly line adds very little value. So why bemoan the loss of assembly line jobs (unless, of course, one is a politician who feeds at the trough of organized labor).

The changes we have witnessed in the work force of the UK or the US correspond to people's desires. Who would rather be a Boeing employee than a hedge fund manager? Or a Washington lobbyist? Is working for IBM that much better than working for Goldman Sachs or GAM? Should we bemoan the fact that the fastest growing segment in the US workforce is 'managers and administrators'? Given that it is the highest paid category, why would we?

Of course, the bears will argue that the 'blue collar jobs' that were lost have been replaced by low-end service jobs (McDonalds, Wal-Mart etc.). We would answer: so what? In a healthy economy, demands for different kinds of workers are changing all the time, and changing so quickly that it is common for specific kinds of workers to find themselves in shortage, or in surplus.

In the labor market, as in any other competitive market, the best indicator of shortages and surpluses are changes in price; in this case, prices are called wages. When workers with particular attributes are in surplus, their real wages fall. Meanwhile, real wages for workers in shortage rise.

In 2001, the average real wage of male college graduates grew by about US$5/hour from 1973, an impressive feat given the large increase in the supply of college graduates. Meanwhile, the real wage of high school graduates remained stable and the real wage of high school dropouts fell by US$3/hour.

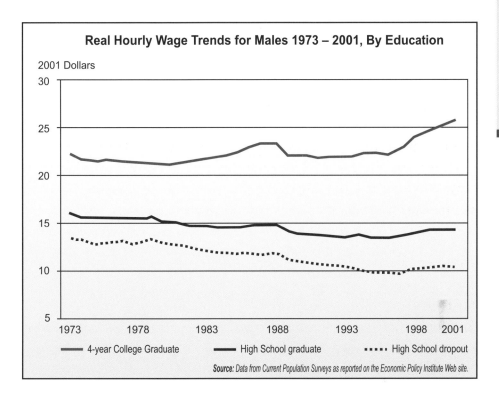

Real Hourly Wage Trends for Males 1973 – 2001, By Education

2001 Dollars

Legend: — 4-year College Graduate — High School graduate ••••• High School dropout

Source: Data from Current Population Surveys as reported on the Economic Policy Institute Web site.

What is impressive in the above data is that over the same period, the number of male college graduates (not to say anything about educated women entering the workforce) grew much faster than the number of male high school graduates or dropouts. The changing occupational structure from Second Wave economy to Third Wave economy created so strong a demand for college graduates that it outstripped its bulging supply.

Alvin Toffler's Third Wave is creating an economy where a vast majority of people are either better off, or keeping par, and a small minority (high school drop-outs) are falling behind. To be sure, this is not good news if one is a 'high school drop-out', but does that mean that the current system is 'unsustainable' or 'on the verge of implosion'? Absolutely not. Which is why we find the bears' Malthusian beliefs to be at odds with the data, common sense, and experience.

The Malthusian belief is unfortunately, more than odd. It is also dangerous for the inherent conclusion of the 'there are not enough good jobs to go around' belief is that we need the government to step in and protect the jobs for us. It also breeds the impression that economic activity is a zero-sum game, while nothing could be further from the truth.

The Milken Institute, in an article written in October 2004, (see *Is Your Job Heading To Bangalore?*) looked at this very issue: *We looked into what happens to a dollar of U.S. corporate spending when a company moves a service job to India. We found that, far from being a zero-sum game, offshoring is a story of mutual gain, benefiting both countries. The receiving economy (India) captures 33 cents, in the form of wages paid to local workers, profits earned by local outsourcing providers and their suppliers, and taxes collected from second- and third-tier suppliers to the outsourcing companies.*

But the gains to the U.S. economy are much larger. The most obvious source of value is the cost savings enjoyed by U.S. companies. For every dollar of corporate spending that moves offshore, American businesses save 58 cents. Companies can reinvest the savings in new business opportunities, pay additional dividends to shareholders, or both. Moreover, because wages are lower in the relevant foreign labor markets, companies can hire more (as well as better-qualified) workers to do the same job, and spend more on supervision and training. Some companies have found that offshore workers are more highly motivated and perform better, particularly in low-skilled jobs that lack prestige and suffer from high turnover at home. One British bank's call-center agents in India process 20 percent more transactions than their counterparts in the United Kingdom and have a 3 percent higher accuracy level.

Consumers benefit, too, as companies are forced to pass on savings in the form of lower prices – much as they now benefit from trade in goods. New research by Catherine Mann of the Institute for International Economics found that the globalization of computer manufacturing has reduced the cost of hardware by as much as 30 percent, thereby boosting demand and adding roughly $230 billion to the U.S. GDP since 1995. Trade in services will do the same. A medical technician in India, for instance, can read an MRI scan at a fraction of the *cost of a comparable analysis in the United States. Transferring that position to India may cause an American technician to be laid off, but lower prices for these lifesaving technologies enable more sick people to receive scans.*

Offshoring yields benefits for the U.S. economy in other ways as well. First, Indian companies that sell the services will also import goods and services – everything from telecommunications equipment to legal and financial expertise. A call center in Bangalore is likely to be filled with HP computers, Microsoft software and telephones from Lucent, and to be audited by PricewaterhouseCoopers.

We estimate that for every dollar of corporate spending that moves abroad, offshore companies buy five cents' worth of goods and services from the United States. On top of that, young Indian workers employed by outsourcing firms buy imported goods. Thanks to these corporate and individual buyers, exports from the United States to India stood at $5 billion in 2003, up from $3.7 billion in 2000. In addition, the U.S. economy benefits because many Indian outsourcing firms are owned in whole or in part by U.S. companies, including General Electric and EDS, that repatriate their earnings. In this way, another four cents returns to the United States.

All told, the direct benefits to the United States from corporate savings, added exports and repatriated profits total 67 cents – twice the benefit to India. But the gains don't end there. Corporate savings may be invested in new businesses in the United States, and that investment will boost productivity as well as creating jobs. Based on historical experience, these new jobs will, on average, add more value than the ones lost: carriage makers were replaced by auto assemblers, and farmers by processed food factory workers.

Indeed, this has been the pattern in recent decades as manufacturing jobs moved offshore.

U.S. manufacturing employment shrank by two million in the past 20 years – but net employment increased by 43 million jobs in other areas, including educational and health services, professional and business services, trade and transport, government, leisure and hospitality, and financial services. Over the same period, domestic manufacturing output increased despite the decline in the number of manufacturing workers, because factories became much more productive. Higher productivity means a higher national income and a higher standard of living.

The pattern is likely to be repeated as jobs in call centers, back-office operations, and information technology services go offshore. Opportunities will appear to redeploy labor and invest capital to generate higher-valueadded occupations will appear. The Bureau of Labor Statistics estimates that between 2000 and 2010, the United States economy will create 22 million jobs (net of jobs lost), mostly in business services, health care, social services, transportation and communications.

The bottom line is simple enough: free trade works in making countries, and consumers, richer. Arguing differently is odd, and dangerous. Claiming that America and Britain are 'losing all the good jobs' is also totally out of touch with reality for it simply refuses to acknowledge the impressive growth in the wealth of the average American family. This impressive wealth is plain to see for any casual visitor to the United States.

The US is a rich country, and rather than trying to find what it is doing wrong, the perma-bears should maybe stop to take a look at what the US is doing right. And what it is doing right is allowing Schumpeterian growth to work its magic.

How schumpeterian growth works – the dark side of the force

Growth can typically be triggered by either an efficient re-organization of talents (we call this Ricardian growth) or new inventions (we call this Schumpeterian growth).

By its very nature, there is no limit to the possibilities of Schumpeterian growth. Man will always come up with new inventions. But these inventions can be as destructive as they are creative. This why Schumpeter called the growth process 'creative destruction'. A quick example: when the fax machine was invented, it spelled the doom of the telex machine (who nowadays has a telex machine in their office?). And when email was invented, the number of faxes sent collapsed…

So how does one promote Schumpeterian growth? We believe that you need at least three very important variables to be in place:

#1- The Right, and the Ability, to Fail

As mentioned above, one man's invention is often another man's ruin; there is a dark side to the force of capitalism. For decades, this dark side of the force has deeply disturbed governments. Firstly, because the dark side appears inhumane. Secondly, because special interest groups threatened by the dark side can be very organised and vociferous (steel industry in the US, construction industry in Japan, farmers and rail workers in France…), bringing to politicians the two things they need (votes & money). Thirdly, because some politicians (namely in

Continental Europe) think they can control for the greater good, with measures & laws, the might of the dark side.

Unfortunately, more often than not, attempts to reduce the effects of the dark side only end up stifling the creative side of the force. Rather than protect jobs, protectionism, market regulation and other measures that prevent competition typically block future inventions and current growth.

European and Asian governments, in their great majority, have been especially guilty of aiming to stifle the dark side. In this light, the steady increase in the difference of productivity growth between the EMU and the US of the past decade is understandable.

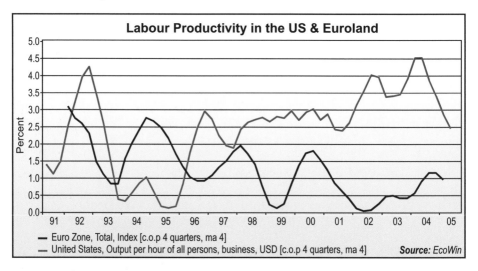

#2- The Legal Protection of Intellectual Property

In the Third Wave society in which we now live, 'value' is increasingly domiciled in intellectual property. Stripped of intellectual property, what would Microsoft be worth? Or Novartis? Or GaveKal? Okay, that last one is probably a stretch since GaveKal is not worth much… but our reader gets our drift. Without a healthy respect for intellectual property, and established legal procedures to defend it, Schumpeterian growth simply cannot flourish.

Establishing the legal framework in which intellectual property can flourish is not easy. It is also an every day task given the constant evolutions in our brave new world; for example, this year, the US Supreme Court had to establish the legality, or not, of music file sharing over the Internet.

Today, intellectual property is decently protected in the Western World but it is not in the greater Emerging Markets. This important difference helps explain, we believe, why so many platform companies are domiciled in the Western World, and so few are in the emerging countries.

This stark difference, however, does not mean that all is rosy for the Western economies, and that good ideas and new processes will only continue to emerge from there. Far from it. In fact, one point of serious concern is that politicians all across the Western World are making the mistakes of their forefathers all over again. Let us explain through the British example.

Following WWII, the British Labour party identified three sectors as the 'growth sectors' of the economy: steel, coal and rail. The government then said that these growth sectors would be better managed by the state. Of course, we know what happened. Today, Britain has no steel, coal or rail industry to speak of. The nationalization of these important sectors prevented ideas from flourishing; creative destruction could not apply.

Today, all over Europe, governments are up to the same trick. While they are happy to leave rail, coal and steel by the side (having destroyed these industries), the new three 'growth' sectors of the future have been identified by governments. They are: education, pensions and healthcare. But in a number of countries, France, Germany, Italy… the governments are saying: these three sectors are the 'chasse-gardée' (protected area) of the government. No one else is allowed to butt in…

This can only mean two things. Firstly, that capital will be wasted (and because these sectors require increasing amounts of capital, the governments will either take it from the taxpayer, or -more likely- finance it through deficits). Secondly, that the growth of ideas, and the pace of creative destruction, will be unfortunately restrained.

#3- The Acceptance of Income Disparity

More than the above, Schumpeterian growth also needs an acceptance by society of the importance of income disparities. Indeed, what is the point of working hard and creating new inventions if a government takes all the profits away in the name of social equality? Any country aiming to promote Schumpeterian growth needs to recognize that the desire to strike it rich remains the greatest motivator. In 1982, Deng Xiao Ping announced that 'to get rich is glorious'; since then, the income of China's city dwellers as increased 14x.

This acceptance of income disparity is probably the hardest thing to achieve in the current political structure of most countries. Why? Because most countries counterpoise the 'social' to the 'unequal' and strive to avoid wide income disparities.

But the refusal to accept income disparities is very destructive. Inherently, it implies that capital is taken from where it is efficient and generating high returns, and distributed where it is not. Such a course of action can only lead to an impoverishment of the greater society; and when the greater society gets poorer, it is the poorest members who suffer the most. Time and again, this has been the experience of socialism.

Trying to prevent the growth of income disparities is also denying an important economic reality: income disparities are a tremendously creative force. As Thorstein Veblen showed in *The Theory of the Leisure Class*, one of the main motors of capitalism is the desire for conspicuous consumption; or, as popular knowledge calls it, the wish to 'keep up with the Jones'. If there are no Jones to keep up with, why get out of bed in the morning?

Looking around the world today, we find that the economies riding Alvin Toffler's Third Wave to the limit of its potential all take a benign view of income disparity, whether the US, the UK, Australia or Hong Kong.

Staying on Hong Kong, the city-state surely ranks as one of the greatest success stories of the past fifty years; no first time visitor to the city fails to be shocked by:

a) How vibrant and wealthy the city is, and

b) The disparities of wealth on display

Hong Kong's economy was destroyed by the Japanese in WWII, destroyed by the UN embargo on trade against China in 1951 and wrinkled by worries over the return of the territory to China. Hong Kong has been hit by typhoons, mud-slides, squatter-camp fires, bird-flu, SARS and massive refugee influxes. Hong Kong has no mines, no oil wells and very little agriculture. Hong Kong also has nowhere to park; yet, the town has the highest ratio of Rolls Royce, Ferrari and Porsche per capita. And Hong Kong also has one of the lowest rates of violent and non-violent crime in the world. How did Hong Kong achieve this success? By encouraging wealth disparity. Hong Kong is a city without minimum wage where the wealthy reap huge rewards.

And yet there is little social tension. Why? Because the unfortunate workers at the bottom of the ladder believe that one day, things will be better. This is a very important point: income disparities are untenable when there is no hope of social advancement. But that is not the case in the US, the UK, Australia or Hong Kong where you find lots of rags to riches stories (e.g. Li Ka Shing). And even more rags to middle class stories.

When the process of creative destruction is allowed to work, we get both income disparity and the ability of people to 'move up'. When income disparity is constrained, the ability of people to climb the social ladder disappears. This is why, in large parts of Europe, 'l'ascenceur social est en panne'.

Where will the growth come from?

As mentioned above, there are two kinds of growth: Ricardian growth (derived from a rational re-organisation of talents) and Schumpeterian growth (derived from new inventions). To promote the Ricardian kind of growth, one needs low trade barriers and industry deregulation. To promote the Schumpeterian kind of growth, one needs low regulations, low taxes, easy access to capital, the ability and right to fail, a strong rule of law with the protection of intellectual property, and an acceptance of income disparities.

So where in the world can we expect to see Ricardian growth? And Schumpeterian growth?

Today, it is visible for all those who care to see that the whole of Asia (and especially India and China), Eastern Europe, Latin America... are going through a massive re-organization of talents. Free-trade pacts are being signed between formerly protectionist nations. Stifling regulations are being taken down. Roads, airports and ports are being built; telecom and electricity cables are being laid etc. An important part of the world is going through a massive Ricardian growth spurt which feels so powerful that it seems unlikely that it could be interrupted by direct government policies (although betting against the destructive powers of politicians is usually a risky bet).

In Western Europe, the US, and in Japan, the Ricardian growth spurt, which came on the back of the creation of the European Union or the NAFTA agreements, has mostly been cashed in, (although, for Europe, the accession to full membership of the new members from Eastern Europe could trigger further efficiency gains). However, because of the restrictions imposed on the free movement of people by most European countries (bar the UK and Sweden), the European Ricardian growth spurt could prove tamer than most expect.

	Ricardian Growth					Schumpeterian Growth					
	Free Move of Goods	Free Move of People	Industry Deregulation	Networking Effect	Total	Low Cost of Capital	Access to Capital	Acceptance of Income Disparity	Intellectual Property Protection	Right to Fail	Total
China	+1	0	+1	+1	+3	+1	+1	-1	-1	-1	-1
India	0	0	+1	+1	+2	+1	-1	+1	0	-1	0
Japan	+1	-1	0	0	0	+1	0	0	0	-1	0
Australia-NZ	+1	+1	0	0	+2	-1	+1	+1	+1	+1	+3
Rest of Asia	+1	0	+1	+1	+3	+1	+1	0	-1	-1	0
Europe	+1	0	-1	0	0	0	+1	-1	+1	-1	0
UK	+1	+1	+1	0	+3	0	+1	+1	+1	+1	+4
Eastern Europe	+1	+1	+1	+1	+4	+1	+1	+1	-1	+1	+3
USA & Canada	+1	0	0	0	+1	0	+1	+1	+1	+1	+4
South America	+1	0	0	+1	+2	-1	-1	+1	-1	-1	-3

The above table brings us back once again to Frederic Bastiat and his premise that, in economic matters, there is always 'what we see, and what we don't see'. What everyone sees today, and is very excited about, is the impressive growth in the emerging markets, whether China, India, Russia, Latin America. This is the 'easy to see Ricardian growth'.

To a large extent, the emerging markets' Ricardian growth spurt relies on important domestic factors such as:

a) Demographic Transformations

Across a number of emerging markets we are witnessing the 'fattening' of age pyramids around the middle. What does this mean? Very simply that while emerging markets do not have a lot of old people (yet), young couples are increasingly having less children. This important social change translates itself into a 'fat pyramid of age' whereas an important majority of people are aged between 15 and 55. This means that most people work, save, consume and that the overall 'dependency ratio' falls. Needless to say, this is great news for growth. Japan and Europe went through such a demographic transition in the 1960 and 1970s. The US did so in the 1980s and 1990s. Now, it is the turn of China, Brazil, Korea…

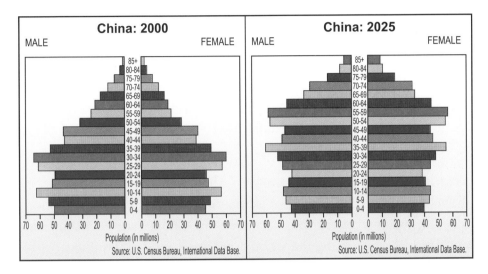

b) The Acceleration Phenomenon

The concept of **'Acceleration'** was first developed by Aftalion, a French economist at the beginning of the XXth century. Aftalion explained that most socio-economic variables are distributed according to the **'normal' law**, the famous bell-shaped curve, affectionately also called the bowler hat. In most developed or developing nations, income is distributed according to a Gaussian pattern, a large percentage of the population having an income close to the 'average' income. There will be few people with a very low income and few with a very high income. At both ends of the curve (the tails), one finds a very small population in percentage. Assuming that, in a given country, the average income in 1985 was US$5,000/year. The number of people earning more than US$10,000 will be, for example, 5%. If, by 1990, this average income goes up to US$8,000 (+60%), the number of people earning more than US$10,000 will not go up by 60%, but by a much larger figure (say 180%).

And this is where the acceleration comes in: when it comes to the buying of certain goods and services, the historical evidence seems to suggest the existence of "thresholds". For example, if the average income in a country is below US$1,000, nobody owns a television; when the income moves above US$1,000, then almost everybody buys one. For the automobile industry, the critical level seems to be US$10,000/year. For university education US$20,000...

So, in the country chosen as an example, when the average income reaches $10,000, the demand for cars will literally explode way beyond the correspondent growth in income. Acceleration works in a very surprising way. Similarly, if the average income falls from US$10,000 to US$8,000, the demand for cars will not decline by 20%, **but will disappear!**

At the same time, if the price of a good falls, then the threshold level falls with it. A quick example. In 1999, there were practically no mobile phone subscribers in China. But as incomes rose and the price of phone calls fell, the market for mobile phones in China evolved from being nonexistent to becoming the world's largest (around 300 million people have mobiles in China).

As incomes rise across emerging markets, various thresholds are crossed and consumption explodes. The boom in consumption is boosted further by the fall in certain prices (electronics, automobiles, etc.). The acceleration phenomenon is what makes deflationary booms possible (more on that later).

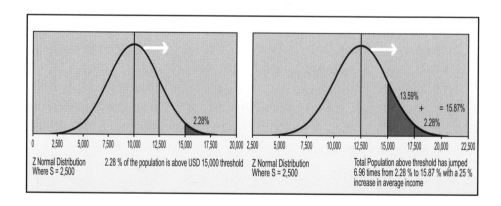

c) Urban Migration

The story of people migrating from a relatively unproductive countryside to more vibrant cities has been a constant theme of both developed and developing markets for decades. But today, this theme is gaining new traction with the massive internal exodus we are witnessing in countries like China.

Over the past decade, China's cities have added approximately 100 million people. Such a rapid urbanisation represents one of the most dramatic population shifts in History. It presents China with both challenges and opportunities. In his last CCP address, President Jiang focused a lot on urbanisation and the potential liberalisation of China's urban policies (today, emigration from the country to the city remains difficult because of the Hukou household registration system). He stated: 'all the institutional and policy barriers to urbanization must be removed and the rational and orderly flow of rural labour guided'.

A deregulation of the housing/registration policy could unleash a new wave of growth around China. It also presents huge challenges to which the government is responding by accelerating deregulation (i.e. home ownership schemes, growth of mortgage industry, deregulation of the utilities industries, relaxation of foreign ownership rules on logistic and transport companies etc.).

Around 80% of China's growth in the past ten years has come from its cities. At the same time, China has added nearly 200 'new' cities. The Asian Development Bank estimates that the number of people in urban areas will expand from 360 million today to 700 million by 2010.

The urban migration currently happening across China and Asia requires massive capital spending. Housing, schools, sewer systems, power plants, transport system... all need to be built.

At the same time, urbanisation across emerging markets brings women into the workforce in ever greater numbers, which, in turn, leads to a fall in birth rates and an overall lower 'dependency ratio' (see above).

d) A Global Re-Organization of Talents

But beyond the well-covered forces behind the current growth spurt of the emerging markets lies another important factor: Asia's Ricardian growth spurt has been given an extra boost by the unprecedented re-organization of talents in the US and across the World triggered by the new 'platform company' business model. As companies relocate an important amount of their production process to cheaper countries around the world, the countries (China, India, Poland…) in question benefit massively. In essence, the Western World is transferring growth from its shores unto the emerging markets' shores.

Unfortunately for the emerging markets, it is not transferring just growth. It is also transferring volatility. So while we should stand in awe of the emerging markets' extremely rapid growth rates, we must also remember that this growth rate could turn out to be more volatile than some expect.

Which then, of course brings us to the question of valuations in the financial markets; for which market should be 'worth' more? A high growth, but volatile market? Or a lower growth, but stable market? The answer to that question might depend on the economic cycle. Owning volatility on the upside is great. But on the downside, it is a far less attractive proposition.

The impressive Ricardian growth spurt developing around the world, but especially in Asia, also raises the question of whether Asia will be able to generate true Schumpeterian growth.

In order to trigger the creative destruction process, you first need entrepreneurs. And in turn, these entrepreneurs need access to capital, at a fair price. For the risks to be worthwhile, our entrepreneurs also need to keep some of the money they will potentially make (i.e. low taxes & no resentment of income disparity) and a system of laws that will protect their invention. They also need to know that, should they fail, their whole lives will not come crashing down.

And it is possibly on that front that Asia is at huge disadvantage. Indeed, in the world today, one finds cultures founded on guilt (the Judeo-Christian World) and cultures founded on shame (Asia). Shame has massive advantages (in that it allows a stronger social cohesion, less crime etc.) but also has one huge inconvenience: it does not allow one to deal with failure.

The shame vs. guilt cultural difference probably explains why, when it comes to Schumpeterian growth, Anglo-Saxons countries today hold such an advantage.

Platform companies do not need our capital

One of the constant laments of the bears is that asset prices are in a 'bubble'; that current valuations are totally out of sync with historical norms. Take the Price to Earnings ratio on the S&P 500, we are told, even after the impressive growth in profits of recent years, and the 2000-2003 bear market, the S&P 500 P/E is still above its historical average; surely this should be a cause for concern?

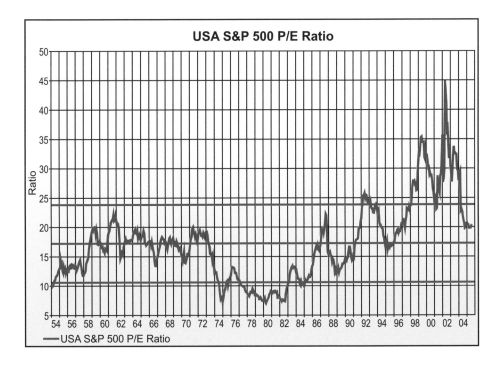

We disagree, for a very simple reason. Namely, that things are different this time. Comparing the S&P to historical valuation is, we believe, not that relevant. What is important is to place the S&P in the context of the present economy. Not the past.

Take Caterpillar and Procter & Gamble as examples. Both are well managed leaders in their respective fields. But Caterpillar operates in a highly cyclical business (earth-moving and construction equipment) while P&G operates in a steady, non-cyclical business (household goods). So, if over the very long term the two companies showed the same growth in earnings, one would expect P&G to trade at a premium to Caterpillar, if for no other reason than P&G earnings were far less cyclical, and far more predictable, than Caterpillar's, and so more attractive to investors.

Now let's take this example and apply it to the broader US economy. As shown above, the US economy today is far less volatile than it was just a decade ago. Surely we must therefore assume that this fall in volatility of the broad economy must have a positive impact on broad asset prices. If it is true at the individual company micro-level, why could it not be true at the broader market macro-level? For some reason that we do not understand, most of the bears are unwilling to make this jump. But nevertheless, the fall in the US economy's volatility is a very positive development for equities.

First we witnessed a collapse in the volatility in the growth of the US economy. Then we witnessed a collapse in the volatility of corporate profits. Then we witnessed a collapse in the volatility of the financial markets (as recorded by the Vix index in Chicago)… Adding one, two and three together, should we be surprised that the valuation on stocks has risen?

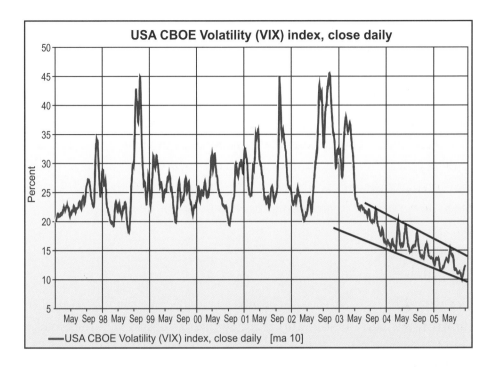

USA CBOE Volatility (VIX) index, close daily

—USA CBOE Volatility (VIX) index, close daily   [ma 10]

Another very important, and recent, development is that Western platform companies need far less capital than their vertically integrated predecessors. Why? Because more often than not, platform companies focus on product development and sales, for which little capital is needed. By keeping just 'variable costs' in-house and outsourcing all the 'fixed costs' and 'inventories' part of the production process, companies are able to operate on very lean budgets. Sometimes platform companies such as Dell or Carrefour can even function on negative working capital (they get their suppliers to provide goods, sell them rapidly, but only pay their suppliers six months later).

To return to IKEA as an example: IKEA never issued shares to the general public; nor did it finance its growth through bond issues. Instead, IKEA financed its growth on its own cash-flows. And this for a very simple reason: when you start off by employing a few designers in an office in Sweden, and rent someone else' s capacity do the heavy lifting for you, how much capital do you really need?

The added twist is that, thanks to the fact that they use up little capital and outsource the cyclical part of their procedures, platform companies offer very high, and stable, returns on invested capital; an attribute that shareholders are usually very fond of.

So we are left with a conflict: as the IKEA example demonstrates, platform companies do not really need the capital that outside shareholders can provide. Meanwhile, shareholders are very eager to 'get a piece' of the growing platform companies. How does this conflict get resolved? Easily; the valuations of platform companies go through the roof.

In the old days, Western companies had to beg, and reward, investors for their capital. Today, since they don't really need outside shareholder's capital, executives can allocate themselves compensation packages that would have been thought impossible a decade ago, fly around in company jets etc. and investors still buy their shares by the truck-load.

This of course does not mean that the valuations (i.e. Google) reached by some of the platform companies are ridiculous and stupid. After all, if, as we believe, Western economies are moving into a world where companies provide higher returns on invested capital, stable profits and if the economy is also more stable, then it makes intuitive sense that these companies should reach valuations higher than they did in the past. More importantly, given the leaner balance sheets and the fall in the economic cycle's volatility, the likelihood of bankruptcy actually shrinks. So equities are now a safer asset class than they used to be.

Another potential factor behind the impressive rise in equity market multiples, and real estate prices, over the past decade could also be the fact that, as mentioned above we live today in a world with an extremely large pool of disposal capital but unfortunately, companies don't really want it. In fact, laws are being changed so that companies can more easily return capital to shareholders (higher dividends in the US, easier LBOs and MBOs in Europe and Asia…), instead of tapping them for it.

So as the excess capital shuffles around, it desperately needs a home. The homes it has found so far have been:

a) Equity markets (where average valuations have risen substantially).

b) Bond markets (where government bond yields are close to record lows and corporate bond spreads are surprisingly tight).

c) Real estate (as mentioned in Chapter 7).

d) Hedge funds (more on that later).

But where the capital is most needed is undeniably in the emerging markets: after all, this is where the big wave of capital-intensive spending is currently taking place (building airports, roads, ports…). Unfortunately, as we write, financial markets are mostly organized to take money from the rich Western saver to deliver it to Western companies. Financial markets are not yet organized to take money from the Western consumer to deploy it in the capital thirsty emerging markets.

Moreover, the appetite of the Western rich saver for the volatile emerging markets might not appear for quite a while. As the Western saver gets older (and he is getting older everywhere), how much appetite will he have for a high growth but highly volatile investment in emerging markets? Will he not feel more comfortable investing at home in the stable growth environment we have described in the above pages? In other words, will he rather not prefer the non-cyclical asset class to the cyclical one? As the French saying goes, 'on ne prete qu'aux riches', and one of the safest rules of banking has always been to only lend money to people who don't really need it.

This preference amongst Western savers for 'low-volatility' returns explains the impressive growth of the hedge fund industry. In fact, in itself, the emergence of this industry out of nowhere is a visible symptom of the fact that: a) we are living in a world with excess capital and b) the tolerance for volatility in the returns of this capital is fairly mild.

The combination of the above two factors has pushed up the valuation of asset prices all over the Western World. We can bemoan it; but we also have to learn to live with it. Such high valuations are part and parcel of the brand new world that we inhabit.

Money pours into hedge funds

With a world awash in capital, we should probably not be surprised that a whole class of investors has emerged with palms outstretched and the assertion that, through them, the capital could find a profitable home. Indeed, the hedge fund industry has grown from practically nowhere a decade ago to managing over US$1tr, if not more, today. This impressive growth obviously has market consequences, and raises some important questions. The first of which is: why do hedge funds make money? And why have the returns been weaker in recent quarters? To answer these questions, we turn to our friend Hunt Taylor who wrote two columns for HedgeWorld back in the Spring of 2005 on this very topic.

What is the value proposition of hedge funds? What function do they serve in society? Virtually every industry, every business, everything that makes money, does so because it makes our lives better. Microsoft makes money because it helps us manage information. Time Warner makes money because it entertains us. Kraft makes money because it feeds us, and General Motors gets us from place to place. Absent a societal function, it's hard to understand why an industry should make large amounts of money for a long time. We need shelter, food, clothing, transportation, etc., and we will pay the entities that provide them to us for our satisfaction. So exactly what value are hedge funds providing to society? And how can we invest in them intelligently if we don't know the answer?

The answer lies inside the structure of the capital and derivative markets. We live, thankfully, in a free-market economy. The reason Starbucks brings us so much Frappachino is that investors are able to provide them with so much capital via the capital markets. And the provision of investment capital is a vital function in society. Is that the function hedge funds provide? Well, no. Not really. They could be short Starbucks. Providing investment capital is the function of the long-only world, which searches out undervalued or growing businesses and either lends them money or takes a stake in their equity. If those funds can own their investment for years, so much the better. That's why society rewards the long-only investor; at least the good ones. They get paid for providing investment capital so the world can fund and grow businesses.

Hedge funds, on the other hand, are both long and short—and long and short and long and short and long and short ad infinitum. And that's just the stocks. They are also long and short and long and short the options, and the stock index futures, and the corporate bonds, and the credit default swaps, and the collateralized debt obligations, and the convertible bonds, and the senior secured loans. And that's just in corporate capital structures. We still have interest rates, commodities and currencies to think about.

*So, if their function is not to provide investment capital, then how are they making our lives work better? Let me suggest this: They may not provide investment capital, but they make the capital markets work better. They make them more liquid. As speculators, they take the other side of derivative contracts from hedgers who need to transfer risk to someone willing to take it on for a price. **In short, they make markets more efficient.***

The business of market efficiency has a history that is as long and lucrative as the markets themselves, and liquidity providers have always been paid, and paid well, for their services. It's just that, traditionally, they existed inside a different set of partnerships than they do today.

Don't kid yourself that the liquidity business is somehow trivial. This was a club where the memberships—seats on exchanges and partnerships at investment banks—cost millions. The business of liquidity is what put the gold in Goldman Sachs and the 'more' in Morgan Stanley. Investment banks and the other great trading partnerships of their day did not attain their wealth by providing investment capital to those who needed it. They attained it by facilitating the provision of investment capital to those who needed it.

Their function dates back to the Middle Ages, when the first merchant banks originated in Italy to facilitate the grain trade. These merchants used to set up benches in the piazzas to lend against the crops ('bank' is a corruption of the Italian banca for bench, and 'bankrupt' is a corruption of the Italian banca rotta, or broken bench). Soon they took to settling the grain loans held by others, discounting the interest charged as a means of getting around the severe sin of usury. In short, they made their money from making the grain market more liquid and efficient.

The practice spread to Germany and Poland, and from there came the great European houses of Schroders, Warburgs, Rothschilds and Barings. In the United States came Goldman Sachs and Morgan Stanley. In Asia there was Jardine Fleming. All of these great houses made their money by facilitating the provision of investment capital to wherever it was needed at the time, from railroad bonds in the 1880s to Japanese warrants in the 1980s. They were getting paid to provide liquidity and risk capital. Let's call this efficiency capital.

These houses all set up proprietary trading operations to help make their various funding operations more liquid for their clients' benefit. They would make short-term markets in government and corporate debt instruments of any maturity to allow their clients market access. They would buy and sell securities relating to IPOs. They would help their clients manage their currency exposures by making short-term markets for them.

*As time went on, they created new and powerful instruments for managing and diversifying financial risk and made markets in them as well. Things like interest rate swaps, credit default swaps, mortgage-backed securities and collateralized debt obligations. And in so doing, they were well-compensated. And that is as it should be. Making markets efficient is quite a legitimate function in society and passes the 'make your life better' test. Thanks to hedge funds, we have deep and liquid markets in everything from crude oil to corporate credit, with a wide selection of hedging and financing options available. **It's not a coincidence that business cycles are smoother today than they were 100 years ago.** Efficiency capital takes all kinds of risk the rest of us don't want. The folks who provide it should be, and are, paid for it.*

As of about 20 years ago, the world was a simpler place, economically speaking. You had investment capital, and you had those who earned their return by providing it. They were the clients of the brokerages (retail and institutional), the mutual funds and the commercial banks (who were lenders). Then you had efficiency capital, which was provided by the investment banks in the OTC markets, the specialists on the stock exchanges and the locals on the commodity exchanges. Twenty years ago, however, two things were very different from today. The ratio of investment capital to efficiency capital was much, much greater. And the world of efficiency capital was 'members only.' The initiation fee was a seat on an exchange or a partnership at an investment bank.

Two evolutions changed the then-prevailing natural order of things. First was the widespread adoption of the limited-partnership structure with the payment of incentive fees for performance: the garden variety hedge fund. Though few could foresee it at the time, this would allow investors to outbid the club members for their top trading talent. Suddenly, the head of the arbitrage desk at Goldman was no longer at the top of the food chain. No matter how many millions the payout was in a good year at Lehman Brothers, 20% of the gain on $500 million (then $1 billion, then $2 billion...) was better. And you could wear jeans to the office, no less. By the mid-nineties, the prop desks had become the equivalent of boarding schools, feeding their top students into the hedge fund industry.

Then the second revolution hit. The partnerships began going public. It turned out shareholders did not have the same appetite for the lucrative, but uncertain, profits that prop trading generated. The idea that an inventory of mortgage backed securities gone sour could cost the company a quarter's earnings was not going to fly in a world where a one cent miss could send a stock plummeting.

Trading was out, fees were in. The culmination of this trend was Sandy Weill shutting down the fabled fixed-income desk at Salomon Brothers. So, by the end of the nineties, we had a wholesale migration of efficiency capital, from one set of partnerships to another. From Goldman Sachs, Jardine Flemings and Salomon Brothers to Moore Capital, Citadel, Renaissance and hundreds of others built in their image. **We had restructured the way the world financed the business of liquidity.**

Which bring us to today. We still have two basic functions for money—investment and efficiency—but hedge funds are now the primary source of the world's efficiency capital. Lots and lots of efficiency capital. More than the world has ever seen.

How much? Well, assets today are estimated at US$1.1 trillion. However, that $1.1 trillion of efficiency capital acts very differently than $1.1 trillion of investment capital. Remember, investment capital is long-only, unleveraged and patient. But efficiency capital? Well, for starters, it's leveraged. There is no way to know precisely how leveraged it is, but 4x would not be close to pushing the envelope. So that makes it act like $4.4 trillion. And it is very active capital. Again, there is no way to know how much, but let's say the global book turns over four times a year. Now it starts to look like $17.6 trillion. In the financial markets, that makes for a very large footprint. $17.6 trillion. No wonder the prime brokers are fond of us. This is not a growing asset class. This is a new world order. This changes the rules of engagement for investors. It is worth taking a moment to think through the possible implications.

First, anyone who can make any money at all will continue to present themselves as a hedge fund. Why? For the money. At 2% and 20%, there is no reason to wrap a strategy in any other structure until investors stop buying. And if you haven't noticed, the investment section of most offering memoranda now allows the manager to operate a chain of dry cleaners, should clean laundry suddenly present a compelling risk-adjusted opportunity. Lest we forget, investor capital is the cheapest source of funding there is. And speaking of cheap capital, any meaningful rise in the global interest rate structure puts lots of hedge funds in trouble. Why? Because the over-abundance of efficiency capital means funds are now chasing very small inefficiencies. And to earn a return on a very small inefficiency, one has to use leverage. For that to work, the money you borrow can't cost more than the small inefficiency you are pursuing. If the cost of money goes up, that particular game ends. And when it does, this is when we are liable to find: 'strategy drift.'…

As Hunt explains, to operate the capitalist system needs both investment capital, and efficiency capital. In the old days, a few privately held investment banks delivered efficiency capital to the market. This meant that, when a market shock occurred, the shock, through the banking multiplier and the fact that the field of efficiency capital was fairly restrained, would often have ripples across the whole economy. Today, the field of efficiency capital is dominated by thousands of hedge funds.

More positively, given the fact that the number of hedge funds has grown exponentially, a situation where a big loss by a hedge fund would trigger a systematic risk, appears less likely today than in the days when the investment banks were providers of efficiency capital. Why? Because thanks to the multiplication of financial products, one hedge fund's loss might be another fund's gain. Also, because the numbers of funds are now so large, the system can easily absorb a few bankruptcies here and there. Meanwhile, the bankruptcy of an investment bank (i.e. Peregrine in Hong Kong in 1997) back in the old days could really shake the system (since there were few of them to begin with).

The flip side of the above coin, as Hunt very correctly points out, is that as the numbers of hedge funds multiply, and the asset under management swell, the returns are dragged lower. The business of efficiency capital has evolved from being a high risk, high reward business to being a low risk, low reward game. As far as the overall economy is concerned, this is a positive development. For investors, however, it makes for less enticing returns.

Deflation: the trump card of financial markets

In previous chapters, we make the case that, thanks to the disappearance of oligopolies and the emergence of the platform company, the world has moved from an inherently inflationary to a deflationary bias. Prices are no longer made on the average cost, but are instead made at the marginal demand. As we have tried to show, the first and immediate implication of this trend is that, all of a sudden, fluctuation in liquidity growth can be absorbed by prices as well as economic activity. In the $MV=PQ$ of Irving Fisher, the P (prices) has become a lot more volatile, especially to the downside, than in the past.

Why does this matter? Because changes in the overall inflationary environment have very deep impacts on financial markets.

The first impact is that, in a deflationary environment, the earnings discount models used by most of us to value equities, stop working; or at least, they stop working for companies with debt on their balance sheets. Why? Because in a deflation, the real cost of debt explodes and renders earnings meaningless. The deterioration of the balance sheet makes the income statement irrelevant. After all, if prices are falling by 10% per annum, then the actual cost of repaying the principal of the debt is increasing by 10% per annum, and this should be subtracted from earnings. In a deflation, earnings will be overstated all the time. Companies with perfectly good earnings might one day be unable to repay their debt.

This painful equation works the other way around; in an inflationary period earnings of companies with debt are understated all the time (because of the cost of maintaining the debt). In such a period assets can be taken over at very attractive prices (which explains the flurry of M&A deals and LBO shops that grew in the United States in the 1970's, 80's and 90's).

Let us take Japan as an example since the country has been mired in deflation since 1990.

One of Japan's biggest problems is that, because of deflation, debt in real terms compounds faster than anyone's ability to repay it. This leads to a severe deterioration in balance sheets and to the kind of forced selling of goods and assets described by Irving Fisher in the *Debt Deflation Theory of Great Depressions.*

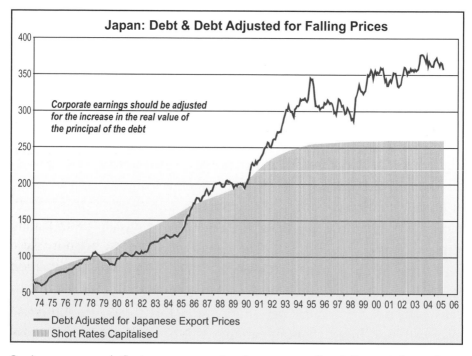

So in a sense, deflation acts as the 'trump card' of financial markets. When it appears, the usual rules go out the window; and for a simple reason: a company whose earnings grow by 20%, but who operates in an economy with price falls of -5% a year, sees the real cost on the principal of its debt rise by 5% a year. This means that some of the earnings have to be taken out to provide for the debt's repayment. The deterioration in the balance sheet can thus take out all of the earnings… and sometimes more.

This explains why discount models in Japan failed as badly as they did in the past fifteen years.

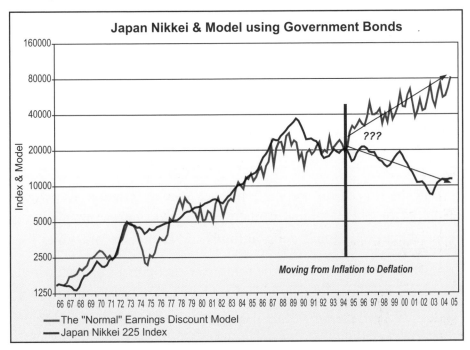

So if we can't use earnings discount models to value equities, what should we do? One possible answer might be given by corporate bond markets. After all, corporate bond investors are very good at spotting deterioration in balance sheets; it's their job. So in a deflationary environment, it probably makes sense to replace risk free rates with quality spreads in our discount models. When spreads tighten, markets can rally, and vice versa.

In Japan, using spreads has worked a whole lot better than using government bonds for a while now.

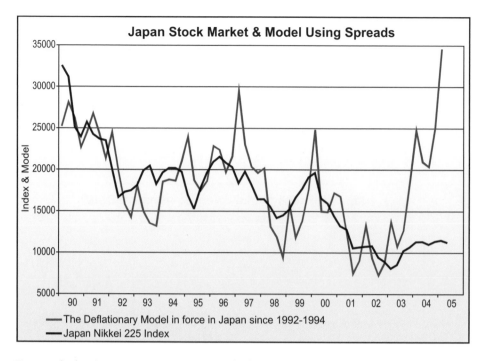

Japan Stock Market & Model Using Spreads

— The Deflationary Model in force in Japan since 1992-1994
— Japan Nikkei 225 Index

Beyond the impact on corporate balance sheets, deflation also wreaks havoc on the book-keeping of many of the most important players in financial markets, namely pension funds and insurance companies.

Companies that have to provide tomorrow's retirement payments hold long dated liabilities -usually linked to the yield of government bonds- and growth sensitive assets (equities, corporate bonds, real estate). When interest rates start falling, and asset prices do not rise, a terrible mismatch occurs.

In the old, inflationary, days, falls in bond yields were not a problem, since they were counterbalanced by a rise in equity markets. So the rise in liabilities triggered by the bond yield were taken care of by a concomitant rise in assets; as a pension fund's liabilities rose, so did its assets. Unfortunately, in the new, deflationary world, **a fall in government bond yields does not lead to a rise but to a retreat of equity markets**. And this is horrible news for pension funds as they are caught in a pincer of a) rising liabilities and b) falling asset values. They then become forced sellers of equities, real estate etc.

This potential mismatch means that the most single important question for the market is neither the direction of economic activity, nor the direction of corporate earnings, but the directions of prices. And it also explains why the Fed came out all guns blazing once the threat of deflation appeared in the system. The Fed knew well enough that any entrenchment in deflationary expectations could lead to a massive pension fund crisis... an unpleasant political development a few years ahead of the retirement of the Baby Boom generation.

The importance of velocity

Unfortunately, deflation's destructive work does not stop at earnings discount models, or at pension funds' accounting assumptions. Deflation also wreaks havoc on most investors' liquidity based macro models, and even on central banks' procedures. Let us explain.

In an inflationary period, keeping cash makes no sense at all since its value is destroyed over time. As such, when central banks add money into the system, the private sector is forced to use, and multiply, this cash rapidly. This simple truth led a number of investors to believe that, following Fisher's $MV=PQ$, any increase in M (money supply) would lead to either an increase in P (prices) or Q (economic activity). And this belief was grounded in sound practice: in every cycle between 1945 and 1995, the above relationship mostly held true… but then it started to break down. Once again, things were different this time around.

The difference was of course that we had moved from an overly inflationary environment to a deflationary one. This meant that central banks could add money into the system and the private sector could elect to sit on this cash. In a deflationary period, the buying power of cash goes up over time, and it pays to accumulate it. So, unlike in an inflationary environment, once deflation emerges, hoarding cash makes economic sense.

This is obviously a very important change, whose first consequence is that all investment models (including our own), which assumed that velocity was a constant, broke down. Instead, changes in the velocity of money became one of the main drivers of financial markets.

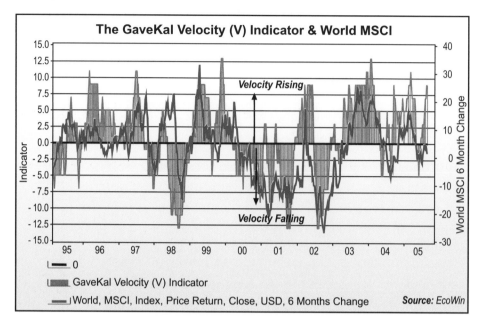

To speak like economists, we would say that **in an inflationary period, there is a natural floor on the velocity of money**; (after a while consumers and companies are forced to spend their money or watch its value disappear). But in a deflationary period, **there is no floor to the velocity of money as hoarding cash is rewarded by a rise in purchasing power.**

An important policy implication of this new economic reality is that that, **if there is no floor on V, then there can be no ceiling on M.** Indeed, trying to restrain the growth of M, at a time of contracting V, can only lead to an implosion in either P or Q (since MV=PQ). Another implication is that central banks can print money, but need to do so at a faster rate than velocity collapses, if they wish for their actions to have an impact on nominal growth.

So if with deflation velocity loses its old constraints, then measuring and anticipating changes in prices and velocity becomes one of the more important tasks faced by both asset allocators and policy makers. Unfortunately, measuring velocity is a thankless task; but as Keynes once said, he would rather be approximately right than precisely wrong. Building velocity models, as we have tried to do in recent years, is critical in an overall deflationary environment. Trying to invest without them is akin to hiking without a map or a compass.

As far as we are concerned, the new map of investing looks something like this:

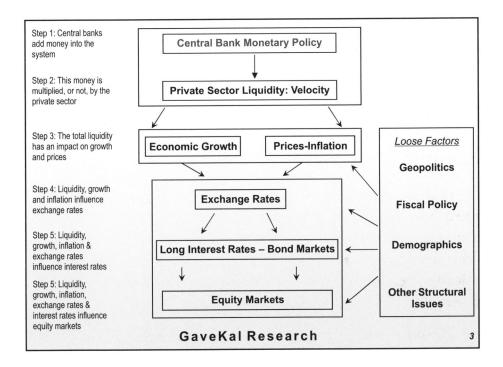

The political impacts of this brave new world

As mentioned above, one of the first implications of the 'platform company' model is that industrial jobs (those close to the hearts of our bearish friends and left wing politicians) in the 'creative world' disappear, only to reappear in Mexico, China etc... Over time, the job market in the developed economies moves to a minority of very creative individuals who work for themselves, and a majority of fellows who work in the service industry for the creative minds and/or the tourists coming in from the industrial world.

This, of course, is a left wing politicians' worst nightmare, if for no other reason that their political parties (whether the Democratic Party, the Labour Party, the Spanish PSOE, the French PS...) all rely heavily on trade unions and organized labor for their funding, and to bring out the votes on election day. No wonder then that the most stringent attacks on globalization and free trade have moved from the First Wave far right to the Second Wave, soft left. As our countries de-industrialize, the left-wing parties lose their bedrock of supports. Take the recent collapse of the AFL-CIO unions in the United States. Who would have thought such an event possible twenty years ago? And who could pretend that this will not have a big impact on the Democratic Party and its ability to win marginal constituencies in Ohio, Pennsylvania or Michigan? With the collapse of the unions, the Democratic Party loses its most important pillar.

Nor is this trend likely to reverse itself, unless of course one turns to protectionism (a fact which might help explain Senator Schumer's rabid anti-China posturing). Moreover, beyond the left-wing parties, the new global re-organization of labour might threaten the very existence of our welfare states. Consider the following.

If we assume that a new part of the world is getting richer (China, India, Russia, Brazil, etc.), then we should probably assume that some entrepreneurs in those countries are making it big. This assumption is not a stretch; there is enough anecdotal evidence to support it (if you doubt that some new entrepreneurs are making it big, go to the Louis Vuitton store in Shanghai on a weekend). If we further assume that, in the countries getting richer, we will start to witness the emergence of institutional savings (pension funds, mutual funds, family offices, etc.), then we should expect big 'savings flows' from the rapidly growing developing world into the Western world. In simple words, the emerging markets' newly rich will feel like investing a part of their newly created wealth in regions of the world where property rights are well protected and where there is a rule of law. The excess trade balances earned by the 'industrial world' have, in fact, little choice but to be reinvested in the assets of the 'creative world'. The pension funds of the 'industrial world' will buy the companies which give their countries work. The successful individuals in the 'industrial world' will also buy real estate in the 'creative world' (because it also happens to be the 'fun world'). This implies that the assets in the 'creative world', and especially the prestige assets will always border on the overvalued. Similarly, given the ability to change a producer if he becomes a little bit too demanding, asset prices in the industrial world will remain a little bit undervalued at all times...

Which brings us to the following point: balance of payments consists of two parts:

1. **The Capital Balance:** if the above holds true, that part will always be positive for countries with well developed financial markets.

2. **The Current Account:** since the two parts add to zero (by construction) it means that the current account in countries with well developed

financial markets (US, UK, HK etc.) should always be in deficit, and massively so…

Taking this a step further, we can assume that, as a result of the constant capital flows, the countries with a well developed capital market will have an overvalued currency and a very low level of long rates. Which in turn leads to robust real estate markets (see chapter 8) and higher asset prices.

We call this 'the dollar asset standard'. Basically, diversified and safe assets in the Western world replace gold as the standard of value in the eyes of new savers in Asia, Latin America or Eastern Europe.

The first implication of this new 'dollar asset standard' is that overvalued currencies, combined with a low cost of money (i.e. low barriers to entry), will prevent anybody in the 'developed financial market world' from making any money in industrial goods. In turn, this development will ultimately force companies in the developed financial market world to move to the 'platform company' business model, specializing in design and in marketing, and letting someone else produce the goods.

But this is where it gets interesting: once they make the switch to the 'platform company' model, a number of companies will likely realize that they should domicile their research and marketing activities in countries with low marginal tax rates, both for their shareholders and their employees.

To some extent, this has already happened in the financial industry. On any given day, the biggest foreign net buyer or seller of US Treasuries is the Caribbean Islands. Now needless to say, the Caribbean islanders are not amongst the world's largest investors; but the hedge funds domiciled there most definitely are. So the 'efficiency capital' of the world, which used to be domiciled in big investment banks in the world's financial centers (whether London, New York, Frankfurt, Tokyo…) has now re-domiciled itself in hedge funds whose legal structures are in the Caymans, Bermuda, the British Virgin Islands etc. The tax revenue on the 'efficiency capital' is now lost for the US, the UK and others…and there is little they can do to gain it back.

And it's not just in finance that this is happening. Hong Kong Land, a property developer is incorporated in Bermuda. Electronic Arts, one of the world's biggest video game designers is incorporated in the Caymans….

As an increasing number of companies move to the 'platform-company' model, it is likely that the top talent will want to work, or at least be taxed, in low tax environments. This will lead to a collapse in tax receipts in countries that do not adjust to this new model. In the new world towards which we are rapidly moving, income taxes will becoming increasingly voluntary and governments will have to get their pound of flesh through property and consumption taxes instead. This should lead to more efficient (i.e. downsized) governments all over the Western World. The platform companies might end up killing off the Welfare State.

In the First Wave world, governments basically provided subjects, who had little say in the matter, a modicum of regalian function (police, army, judges). With the Second Wave, governments started to branch out from their regalian functions and provided citizens with income redistribution, education, pensions, healthcare, unemployment insurance etc. But in the Third Wave world, will governments still be able to provide 'prosumers' with all of the above services? How will they pay for them? In the Third Wave world in which platform companies operate, taxes will increasingly become voluntary. Hereby implying that governments will have to compete with each other to provide the best services at the lowest possible costs to attract the world's best platform companies, and their workers. Over time, this should mean that governments that provide the most efficient regalian functions, and at the lowest possible cost (Hong Kong? Singapore? …) will thrive. Will others go bankrupt?

How do we invest in this brave new world? Is indexing the answer?

In the previous pages we have asked a lot of questions, and tried to provide concise and clear answers. Yet of all the questions we asked, this last one is possibly the only one of most interest to our reader; how do we invest in this brave new world of ours? Is the answer, as some argue, to throw our hands up, admit that the world is too complicated for us to understand, and entrust our capital to computers? In other words, go out and put all of our money in index funds? We do not think so.

There is little doubt that indexation is the cheapest way of capturing the attractive long-term returns offered by the capitalistic system. From there, it would be easy to deduce that one should have part, if not all, of one's portfolio indexed. But this conclusion would be wrong, as indexation works on three basic premises, legitimate at the micro-economic level, but chaos inducing on a macro scale. They are:

1. Active money managers allocate capital according to what they perceive to be the future marginal returns on invested capital (ROIC).

2. Few active (stock selection) money managers will outperform the indices over the long term.

3. Very few active money managers will add value through asset allocation. Massively diverging from indices does not work.

These three founding principles are fine on their own but **internally contradictory**. Indeed, the system can work only as long as active money managers attempt to do the job for which they are paid i.e. allocating capital according to what they perceive to be the future ROIC in the different investments which they consider at any given point in time. Most of them will fail, but the process of screening for future ROIC is vital for the well being of the capitalistic system. Winners emerge, losers collapse. In this creative destruction (or is it destructive creation?), capital is allocated efficiently through a constant system of trial and error.

To put it in another way: the active money managers (and their clients) support most of the costs; the indexers get most of the rewards. Without a doubt, this is what happened in the 1980's and 1990's. So why did it stop working? Easy. The active money managers, chastised by years of underperformance, were forced to become 'closet indexers'. In January 2000, some of our clients in the City got fired from their fund management job for refusing to own France Telecom or Nokia.

And this behavior brought the entire system down. The business of money management had become so big after a decade long bull market that it had been taken over by 'professional people', advised by consultants. Often, these management teams wanted to conserve, and not create. They were accountants, not entrepreneurs. The management of the firms (not money managers themselves anymore) attempted to reduce the unpredictability of the results of their money management teams by preventing them from taking risks. And risk was defined as a deviation from the index against which the money managers were measured (hence the introduction of 'risk controls', 'tracking errors' etc.).

What were the results of these changes? Initially, important changes in the industry. Later, a massive bear market. To put it succinctly, indexation became a victim of its own success for two reasons.

The first consequence of the move towards closet indexing was that money management evolved from being an exciting and intellectually stimulating business to a boring and mind-numbing number-crunching game. This was a blow to a number of individuals who had spent their lives in the industry; it also meant that money management started to attract a different type of character than it did a decade ago (i.e. originals, free-thinkers, crazy people).

The second, most harmful consequence is that capital started to be allocated according to size, rather than future returns on invested capital. Indeed, relevant indices are all, for the most part market weighted. In simple English - which we don't always understand but profess to speak – this means that investments get allocated to companies according to their stock market size. This allocation of capital according to size was tried out before, and, the last time we checked, the Soviet Union was not doing that well.

Indeed, in an ironic twist of history, in its hour of triumph over communism, capitalism devised a **socialist** way of allocating capital. All of a sudden, investors across the capitalist markets decided that it was better to invest in companies according to their size than according to their marginal returns on invested capital. The capital allocators did this, supposedly, for the benefit of workers (the future retirees). Unfortunately, if this system were pushed to its logical conclusion, the workers would be left holding the bag. As the Holy Catholic Church states, and history shows, the road to hell is paved with good intentions.

Behind this switch of allocating capital according to size, one finds hundreds of studies, published by thousands of scholars and consultants (and financed by Wall Street dollars) justifying indexation. But what the studies do not acknowledge is that the data on which conclusions are drawn represent a period where active management was both truly active and dominant. In other words, indexing represents a form of black box investing; but black box investing can only work if:

a) volumes are kept fairly low,

b) nobody knows that a black box is operating (see the disaster behind the portfolio insurance of 1987) and,

c) nobody knows how the black box works.

Clearly, none of these three rules apply to indexing.

The more money flows into indexation strategies, the more capital gets invested according to size, and the more capital is misallocated. This can only lead to a lower return on invested capital, which, in turn, can only lead to a lower growth rate and, more often than not, to huge disturbances in price levels. As the late 1990s craze showed, indexation is a guarantee for capital to be wasted, which automatically leads to lower growth and lower long-term returns on the stock markets. So we could have a very paradoxical result: indexers might keep outperforming but the long term returns of the stock markets will fall, as a sign that the economy's structural growth rate is falling.

Once again, we need to remember Bastiat's law: 'there is always what you see and what you do not see'. We shall see the underperformance of active money managers. We shall not understand the result of them being forced to index: the long term declines in the rates of returns in the stock markets. A study of the1998-2003 bull and bear market illustrates perfectly what we are trying to prove. In 1999, we had the perfect case of a stock market going up strongly in index because a few big stocks were bought massively, first by the indexers (which is fine), and then by the closet indexers (which is suicidal).

Being both natural optimists and fervent believers in an efficient free-market, we cannot believe that the system is bent on self-destruction. We do not want to admit that, because the money management industry has become too sophisticated and too risk averse for the good of the economic system it is supposed to serve, we will have to face years of bear markets and sub-par growth. The market will find a way to triumph.

And maybe it has. Indeed, as we all know, experienced money managers have been leaving the bigger firms in hordes over the past few years to set up their own hedge funds. Interestingly, the main characteristic of a hedge fund is that it aims to allocate capital efficiently, and that it puts its neck on the block.

Capital is flowing in huge amounts to this new breed of managers. By creating a class of absolute return oriented money managers, the system has effectively recreated the cautious money managers of yesteryear, bent on delivering steady and understandable returns. One hopes that these fellows, willing to do their jobs (i.e. incur a high tracking error) will take the indexers and closet indexers to the cleaners. The more (and quicker) they do it, the better for the long-term health of our economic systems.

Beyond the growth of hedge funds, another solution might be to break up the big pension funds, and return the monies to their legitimate owners. These owners, who (in the Western World at least) tend to be more financially savvy than their forefathers, would then select their own money managers. The big money management firm would then have to deal with the public in general; a public who tends to define risk as 'losing money', and not as a divergence from the index.

And here, once again, the revolution we are witnessing in the organizational structures of businesses in the Western World might lead to that result anyway. Indeed, as the workforces in Western economies move from massive industrial organized companies to small, service-oriented firms, the ability to draw pension contributions from a large number of workers disappears. With the death of the large, top-down, integrated companies, how can the large pension funds survive? Our answer: they won't. Which means that, along with a rethink of our welfare states, we also need to rethink how retirement in the Western world will be funded.

In the meantime, if we should not give all of our capital away to computers, should we follow the current trend and pile into hedge funds?

How do we invest in this brave new world? Are hedge funds the answer?

As mentioned in Chapter 14, so much money has poured into hedge funds in recent years that the world might now be swimming in too much 'efficiency capital'; which, of course, means that the returns on 'efficiency capital' could end up being somewhat disappointing.

But beyond this initial concern, we are also somewhat uncomfortable in the growing trend amongst institutional investors in quantifying 'hedge funds' as an independent asset class which needs to be part of a portfolio alongside bonds, equities, cash or commodities. And this for a simple reason: hedge funds are extremely diverse and it is hard to find two that are alike in styles, outlook, strategies and approach. So it is hard to see what makes 'hedge fund' an independent asset class on their own. After all, how do hedge funds relate to the economic cycle? To the liquidity cycle? Given the lack of historical data, and the constant transformation of the hedge fund world, it is hard to come up with concrete and definite answers to the above questions.

The one thing we can do, however, is look at how hedge funds have historically made money, and whether they will be able to continue making money in the brave new world that we have described in the above pages.

Breaking down the fields of hedge fund activity (merger arbitrage, convertible bond arbitrage, index arbitrage etc.) it seems to us that a typical hedge fund makes money in one of three ways:

1- **Through 'Return to the Mean' Strategies:** The first way to make money in the financial markets is to buy what is undervalued/oversold and to sell what is overvalued/overbought and wait for the asset price in question to return to its historical mean. This is the strategy adopted by most 'value' managers, but also frequently a number of 'macro-funds', 'distressed-debt', 'special-situations', etc.

2- **Though Momentum Based Strategies:** The second way to make money in the financial markets is to identify a trend and get in (and out) at the right time. Most money managers do try to invest following momentum, but it is especially prevalent amongst 'growth' investors, 'macro-funds', and 'long/short' hedge funds.

3- **Through Carry Trade Strategies:** The third and final way to make money in the financial markets is to play intelligently the yield curve (i.e. borrow at low rates and lend at higher rates...and hope that the markets remain continuous). Most of the 'arbitrage' type of hedge funds run some kind of carry trade.

Needless to say, a money manager is never limited in his choice. In fact, some of the best money managers we have met over the years usually play two, or even three of the above strategies at the same time. However, reviewing the broader hedge fund indices, it seems that none of the above strategies have worked that well in recent quarters. Why could this be?

One possible explanation, as mentioned by our friend Hunt Taylor above, is that there is now simply too much money chasing too few opportunities.

Another explanation might be that the collapse in the volatility that we have witnessed, while good news for our global financial systems is bad news for all the return to the mean investors. Indeed, most hedge fund managers will tell us: 'I don't care if the market goes up, or down, as long as it moves. The worse thing that can happen to me is for the darn thing to be stable'... but if the new organizational structures adopted by

Western companies strip the volatility of earnings away, should we not assume the Western financial markets will be less volatile? And if so, will that not mean that return to the mean opportunities will be harder to come by?

And it's not like carry-trade managers have it that much better. Indeed, in the world we have described, in which prices can take the brunt of the cyclical adjustment just as well as growth, we would expect yield curves in Western countries to be either slightly positive (when economic activity accelerates) or slightly inverted (when economic activity decelerates). Throughout the great capitalist expansion of the XIXth century, interest rates remained low, and yields curves were either flat or inverted. And in such an environment, it is hard to see how carry-trade players make as much money as they did in the glory days of the anti-inflation, steep yield curves of the 1980s and 1990s.

Which brings us to momentum strategies, which tend to always work well, until they don't, with the trigger often being a change in the global liquidity environment. This implies that the best momentum managers one should own are probably macro managers, as they are most likely to perceive the important changes in the overall investment environment. Another way to own momentum based strategies is of course to simply buy index funds... but we have said enough about that already!

So what should we do with our money?

Our first gut reaction would be to say that we have several options.

The first option would be to give it to the consumer: If, as we argue above, the growth of outsourcing leads to higher and more stable returns on invested capital, lower volatility in the economic cycle, higher productivity amongst workers and higher disposable incomes for consumers, then the obvious thing to overweight is consumer plays (retail, consumer finance etc.). But then the question becomes 'to what extent are the consumer's gains from the outsourcing trends already reflected in asset prices'? We would argue that, in countries like the US, Australia or the UK, we are most likely in the 6th or 7th inning of a 9 inning game. However, in other countries (Japan? Singapore? Sweden?) the benefits derived from the adoption of the platform company model are only just starting to have a macro-impact. Overweighting the consumer in such countries makes a lot of sense.

The second option is to buy scarcity assets. One of the major characteristics of the new cycle described on previous pages is that 'those who have, get more'. Indeed, in the second wave economy, the usual economic law of decreasing marginal returns was prevalent. For example, at some point, producing an extra car was an uneconomic expense for General Motors. However, in the 'Third Wave' world, marginal costs of production can often be close to nil; in fact, additional users often add extra value to a product. For a number of companies, or industries, we are now facing a law of 'increasing returns' where first-movers and important players are able to squeeze providers and capture entire markets (i.e. E*Bay, Microsoft, Wal-Mart, IKEA etc.).

In such a world, the poor get richer through falling prices, low interest rates and rising disposable incomes. The rich get insanely rich by capturing entire markets where the marginal cost of production is zero; (what does an extra user of Google cost the company?) Income disparities then grow, but the overall society prospers.

The first consequence of the rich getting even richer is that scarcity assets (fine wines, nice art, houses in Aspen, in Kensington, on the Peak etc.) get bid up to levels no-one had thought possible just a few years ago. So in this brave new world, overweighting scarcity assets makes sense. But there again, we are forced to confront the question of 'how much is in the price'? Looking at prices in Kensington, on the Peak, or in the Hamptons, one might answer: 'all of the above, and then some!' When markets feel as overstretched as some do, it really becomes a dangerous timing game…

The third option is to provide capital to emerging markets. If the heavy duty capital spending now takes place at the periphery, it would make sense for capital allocators to build operations there and deploy more capital to emerging markets. The problem is, of course, that results there are bound to be extremely volatile if for no other reason than:

a) Emerging markets are very liquidity sensitive and

b) If the US economy has exported part of its volatility, this volatility had to go somewhere… and it went to the profit margins of companies operating in periphery countries (China, India, Mexico, Poland etc.).

This means that exposure to emerging markets has to be timed efficiently to coincide with the cycle (incidentally, this is what we aim to do with the GaveKal Asian Balanced Fund).

A fourth and final option is to buy platform companies everywhere. Given that platform companies offer higher, and more stable, returns on invested capital one would expect them, over the long term, to outperform. But then the question obviously becomes the extent to which a platform companies' financial prospects are already reflected in the price? For some (E*Bay? Dell? Google?) most of the prospects might already be discounted; so the inordinate profits might have to be found in 'old business model' companies that, like Apple, successfully transform themselves into efficient 'platform companies' (P&G? Glaxo?). Inordinate profits might also be found in 'platform companies' where the management decides that, given its low need for capital, the company (or more importantly its management) is better off taking the company private. In the coming years, we would not be surprised to see a spate of large management buy-outs, especially if multiples keep on contracting. In turn, this should boost investment banking stocks.

Now, needless to say, any of these recommendations would likely scare a potential investor away since all of the above asset classes have been running higher for quite a while. Which then begs the question of how does one hedge one's risk? And just like we found three ways to make money in the markets (return to the mean, momentum, carry trade), we find three ways to manage the risk in investment markets.

#1: Diversification: Undeniably, this is the oldest way of managing risk. By spreading one's eggs across several baskets, one can hope to withstand most shocks. However, for a diversification to be successful, it must be well implemented and thought through (more on that later).

#2: Insurance (i.e. credit default swaps, options, portfolio insurance etc.): the advantages here are that by buying insurance one knows exactly one's cost; and having insurance can help one sleep at night. The inconvenience is that while it is easy to buy puts on certain asset classes (i.e. S&P 500) to protect a portfolio on the downside, buying insurance on more exotic asset classes is nearly impossible (i.e. options against falls in high end real estate? Portfolio insurance in China? Credit default swaps on Indonesian credit?).

#3: Hedging (i.e. selling futures, shorting stocks etc.): this is the way that most hedge funds keep their exposure to wide fluctuations in the financial markets to a minimum. But as above, one is confronted by the same problem of the lack of financial instruments. How does one short high-end real estate? Or even Indonesian government debt? Another problem with shorting is of course that, unlike insurance, one ends up with the potential for limitless losses. A dangerous proposition at a time of accelerating creative destruction. If one gets the reading on the destruction-creation equation wrong, one can be cleaned out!

So out of the three ways to manage the risk, our natural inclination is to pick the first one; through intelligent diversification one is able to withstand most market shocks. And this simple idea brings us back to the very premise on which GaveKal was founded, namely that investing money is not as much about picking winners as it is about avoiding losers. An investment strategy that can identify the losers, and diversify amongst remaining asset classes will always outperform over the medium and long term.

Building an efficient portfolio in our brave new world

A large majority of asset allocators spend most of their time trying to determine how strong, or weak, economic growth in the months, quarters, or years ahead will be. But only focusing on growth offers a very incomplete picture of the potential risks and rewards in the system. As we have tried to show in previous pages, changes in prices can be just as important as changes in economic activity, in driving investment performance. So important in fact, that we believe it is necessary to characterize investment environments according to changes in both prices and economic activity.

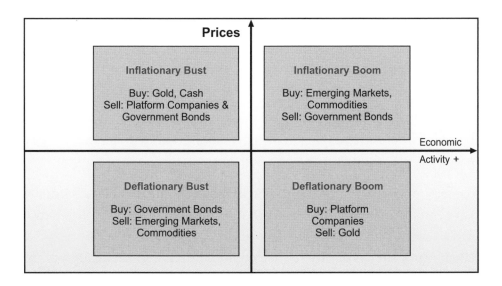

And when we do, we come up with the above grid, which clearly highlights that investors can face one of four different investment scenarios.

The first investment scenario is the 'inflationary bust', also known as stagflation. This investment environment was prevalent in the last 1970s and early 1980s. Stagflation is triggered by excessive government spending monetized by a carefree central bank. Warning signs of such a scenario are an increase in government spending as a % of GDP and excessive growth in monetary aggregates. In such an environment, the best thing to own is gold since investors will tend to flee from their rapidly depreciating currencies into the relative safe-harbor which gold represents.

The second investment scenario is the inflationary boom. This is the investment environment that has been the most prevalent since the end of the Second World War, and as such the investment environment upon which most of the world's financial institutions base their strategy. However, as we have tried to argue in this book, the fact that the world has mostly known inflationary booms in the past decades does not mean that we will continue to go through inflationary booms in the coming decades; investment rules could change very rapidly.

The biggest beneficiaries of an inflationary boom are always the price-sensitive producers. As prices accelerate, they see their sales in both volume and value go through the roof, and their profit margins rise even more. In today's world, the most price sensitive producers tend to be found in either the emerging markets, or commodities. In an inflationary boom, overweighting those two asset classes makes a lot of sense.

The reason we enter into an inflationary boom in the first place is usually that central banks push too much money into the system. As the central banks realize that they might have added a little too much rum to the Punch bowl, they typically reverse course and tighten monetary policy. More often that not, this means that government bond markets face serious headwinds in inflationary boom periods.

The third possible scenario is the deflationary boom. Annoyingly, in casual conversation, most economists and politicians frequently use deflation and depression as synonyms; probably because the last great depressionary period in the 1930s was associated with falling prices. This is a mistake, for falling prices can sometimes be met by booming economic activity. Looking in past history, capitalism has gone through many cycles of falling prices and booming economic activity.

Indeed, we must not forget that what matters first and foremost for companies are sales. Managing a business when nominal sales are rising is easy; managing a business when nominal sales are falling is a nightmare.

Sales are the product of volumes sold against prices achieved. So saying that we are in a deflationary period is only making a comment on the price side of the equation; it offers no information as to the volume side of the equation, or, more importantly, to total sales. In fact, when prices fall, we can face one of two situations:

a) Volumes rise faster than prices fall (elasticity to prices >1) and we are then in a deflationary boom or

b) Prices fall faster than volumes, or both fall together (elasticity to prices <1), in which case we are then in the very ugly and nasty deflationary bust.

Most of our research, and history, leads us to believe that a deflationary boom is the natural state of capitalism, and while this natural state might be interrupted by short, or long, waves of deflationary busts, inflationary busts or inflationary booms, over the very long term, the deflationary boom will prevail.

More importantly, we believe that after twenty-five years of inflationary busts (US 1972-1982), followed by inflationary booms (US 1983-2000), followed sometimes by deflationary busts (Japan since 1990, Asia between 1997 & 2003), we are about to enter a global phase of deflationary boom. The problem, of course, is that no one has a clue as to how to invest money in a deflationary boom…and basing investment decisions on past cycles won't help much (not that we are trying to talk ourselves out of a job!).

Looking back through the deflationary booms of the XIXth century, and the deflationary boom prevalent in the US since the mid 1990s, we find that the usual winners have been:

a) The currency (since its purchasing power rises),

b) The local consumer,

c) Local financials, especially banks,

d) Real estate, especially at the very high end,

e) Anyone who produces goods with an elasticity to prices and an elasticity to revenues greater than 1.

As we see it, in a deflationary boom, the best thing to own are companies able to expand, or contract their operations rapidly; and at the risk of beating a dead horse, this means owning platform companies.

The fourth and final investment environment is of course the deflationary bust. Probably the worst kind of investment environment as every single asset class goes down in price save one: high quality government bonds.

To enter into a deflationary bust, one must have the returns on invested capital fall below the cost of capital for a substantial period of time. Looking back through history, such a collapse usually only occurred when governments stomped their heavy boots onto the markets. To move into a deflationary bust, governments need to commit one, or several of the following cardinal sins:

- An increase in taxation

- An increase in regulation

- Protectionism

- A war

- Following too tight a monetary policy

Any of the above mistakes can lead returns on invested capital to plummet and/or the cost of capital to rise inordinately. When those mistakes are made, investors should load up on the government bonds of countries with healthy balance sheets and undervalued currencies, for the coming quarters will likely prove to be rough.

Putting it all together, we would therefore argue that a private investor should build his portfolio around four key asset classes:

- Cash or Gold,

- Emerging Markets or Commodities,

- Platform Companies,

- High Quality Government Bonds.

An investor who does not feel confident in taking a view on the direction of prices or economic activity could just split his money four ways between the four asset classes, head off to the beach, and rebalance once a year. Over the long term, we believe his performance would most likely be surprisingly good.

Investors who, like us, have not learnt from their mistakes and continue to believe that they can efficiently time markets, could meanwhile decide to allocate their capital to one, two, or three of the above strategies, eliminating the scenario whose odds appear the smallest.

For what it's worth, today we believe that the odds of a structural inflationary bust are very small, and those of a deflationary boom quite high; therefore, in our brave new world, keeping an overweight position in platform companies makes sense.

The End.

ISBN-13: 978-988-98790-1-3
ISBN-10: 988-98790-1-8